Hungarians in Michigan

DISCOVERING THE PEOPLES OF MICHIGAN
Arthur W. Helweg, Russell M. Magnaghi, and Linwood H. Cousins, Series Editors

Ethnicity in Michigan: Issues and People
Jack Glazier and Arthur W. Helweg

French Canadians in Michigan
John P. DuLong

African Americans in Michigan
Lewis Walker, Benjamin C. Wilson, and Linwood H. Cousins

Albanians in Michigan
Frances Trix

Jews in Michigan
Judith Levin Cantor

Amish in Michigan
Gertrude Enders Huntington

Italians in Michigan
Russell M. Magnaghi

Germans in Michigan
Jeremy W. Kilar

Poles in Michigan
Dennis Badaczewski

Dutch in Michigan
Larry ten Harmsel

Asian Indians in Michigan
Arthur W. Helweg

Latinos in Michigan
David A. Badillo

South Slavs in Michigan
Daniel Cetinich

Discovering the Peoples of Michigan is a series of publications examining the state's rich multicultural heritage. The series makes available an interesting, affordable, and varied collection of books that enables students and lay readers to explore Michigan's ethnic dynamics. A knowledge of the state's rapidly changing multicultural history has far-reaching implications for human relations, education, public policy, and planning. We believe that Discovering the Peoples of Michigan will enhance understanding of the unique contributions that diverse and often unrecognized communities have made to Michigan's history and culture.

Hungarians in Michigan

Éva V. Huseby-Darvas

Michigan State University Press

East Lansing

⊚ The paper used in this publication meets the minimum requirements
of ANSI/NISO Z39.48-1992 (R 1997) (Permanence of Paper)

Michigan State University Press
East Lansing, Michigan 48823-5245

Printed and bound in the United States of America

08 07 06 05 04 03 1 2 3 4 5 6 7 8 9 10

LIBRARY OF CONGRESS CATALOGING-IN-PUBLICATION DATA
Huseby-Darvas, Éva V.
Hungarians in Michigan / Éva V. Huseby-Darvas.
p. cm. — (Discovering the peoples of Michigan)
Includes bibliographical references and index.
ISBN 0-87013-644-5 (pbk. : alk. paper)
1. Hungarian Americans—Michigan—History. 2. Hungarian Americans—Michigan—Social
conditions. 3. Immigrants—Michigan—History. 4. Michigan—Ethnic relations. 5.
Michigan—Social conditions. I. Title. II. Series.
F575.H95 H87 2002
977.4'00494511—dc21
2002153200

Discovering the Peoples of Michigan. The editors wish
to thank the Kellogg Foundation for their generous support.

Cover design by Ariana Grabec-Dingman
Book design by Sharp Des!gns, Inc., Lansing, Michigan

COVER PHOTO: Women from the Hungarian Reform Church of Allen Park
preparing dough for a csiga noodle-making demonstration at Michigan State
University's Michigan Folklife Festival, East Lansing, August 1989
(photo courtesy of Robert M. Darvas).

Visit Michigan State University Press on the World Wide Web at:
www.msupress.msu.edu

To Mariska Leleszi and other helpful and kind members of the Hungarian American community in Michigan—with appreciation and love.

Hálás köszönettel és szeretettel.

ACKNOWLEDGMENTS

Many people helped me during the research, writing, editing, and completing of this project. While they are certainly not responsible for either the contents or the conclusions of this work, a number of people from the American Hungarian community in Michigan deserve my gratitude and special recognition for offering their invaluable assistance at various stages of research. They include Mrs. Linda Enyedi, Dr. Péter Kovalszki, Mrs. Mariska (Mary) Leleszi, Mr. Tamás Markovits, Mrs. Ursula Markovits, Mrs. Györgyi Míkó, Mrs. Violet Misángyi, Mrs. Erzsike Veres, Mr. Zoltán Veres, Mrs. Piroska Zoltán, and Mr. Sándor Zoltán. I am particularly appreciative to Dr. Péter Kovalski for thought-provoking and fruitful discussions, and also for calling my attention to some 2000 census data.

In addition, I am grateful for the kind help of the former pastors of the American Hungarian Reformed Church in Allen Park, Michigan, particularly Bishop and Mrs. Dezső Ábrahám and Pastor Imre Bertalan and their staffs, as well as four priests, formerly of the Holy Cross Roman Catholic Church in Delray, Michigan, Fathers Csorba Domonkos, Vendel Pócsai, Julius Fűzér, and Vazul Végvári and their staff.

At various phases of writing, my good friends and colleagues György Csepeli, Miklós Kontra, and Fran Markowitz read the manuscript and offered ever-keen eyes, constructive criticism, and valuable suggestions. I am indebted for their help. I thank my fellow anthropologist, the editor of this important series, Arthur Helweg, for his continued encouragement throughout the long gestation of this project.

Finally, I thank Robert M. Darvas for *really being there*. Not only was he helping with all my work by taking photographs, but he was standing by throughout the years of research and the months of writing and rewriting, readily giving me his constant love and support.

The present work relies on a number of research projects that I conducted between 1979 and January 2002. I appreciate the generous support I got from time to time from the International Research and Exchanges Board (IREX); the American Council of Learned Society (ACLS); NEA Research Grant No. RO-20663-84; and the University of Michigan's Alcohol Research Center.

SERIES ACKNOWLEDGMENTS

Discovering the Peoples of Michigan is a series of publications that resulted from the cooperation and effort of many individuals. The people recognized here are not a complete representation, for the list of contributors is too numerous to mention. However, credit must be given to Jeffrey Bonevich, who worked tirelessly with me on contacting people as well as researching and organizing material.

The initial idea for this project came from Mary Erwin, but I must thank Fred Bohm, director of the Michigan State University Press, for seeing the need for this project, for giving it his strong support, and for making publication possible. Also, the tireless efforts of Keith Widder and Elizabeth Demers, senior editors at Michigan State University Press, were vital in bringing DPOM to fruition.

Otto Feinstein and Germaine Strobel of the Michigan Ethnic Heritage Studies Center patiently and willingly provided names for contributors and constantly gave this project their tireless support. Yvonne Lockwood of the Michigan State University Museum has also suggested and advised contributors.

Many of the maps in the series were prepared by Gregory Anderson at the Geographical Information Center (GIS) at Western Michigan University under the directorship of David Dickason. Additional maps have been contributed by Ellen White.

Other authors and organizations provided comments on other aspects of the work. There are many people that were interviewed by the various authors who will remain anonymous. However, they have enabled the story of their group to be told. Unfortunately, their names are not available, but we are grateful for their cooperation.

Most of all, this work is a tribute to the writers who patiently gave their time to write and share their research findings. Their contributions are noted and appreciated. To them goes most of the gratitude.

ARTHUR W. HELWEG, *Series Co-editor*

Contents

Introduction

From her beacon-hand
Glows world-wide welcome; her mild eyes command
The air-bridged harbor that twin cities frame.
"Keep, ancient lands, your storied pomp!" cries she
With silent lips. "Give me your tired, your poor,
Your huddled masses yearning to breathe free,
The wretched refuse of your teeming shore.
Send these, the homeless, tempest-tossed to me,
I lift my lamp beside the golden door!"

—Emma Lazarus, "The New Colossus"

When Emma Lazarus wrote these often-cited lines in 1883, Hungarians were just beginning to flock to the United States in increasing numbers. Between 1880 and the First World War, "a million and a half staggered out," lamented Attila József, one of the most sensitive and outstanding poets of twentieth-century Hungary.[1]

The majority of emigrants from that first wave were rural Hungarians who left their homeland primarily for economic reasons, and not necessarily "to breathe free." They wanted to work hard, live frugally, and save enough to return to their home village and live in comfort ever after. Even though they were industrious and thrifty, they rarely realized their dreams. Only a small percentage permanently returned to their homeland. Some became "commuters," circular or

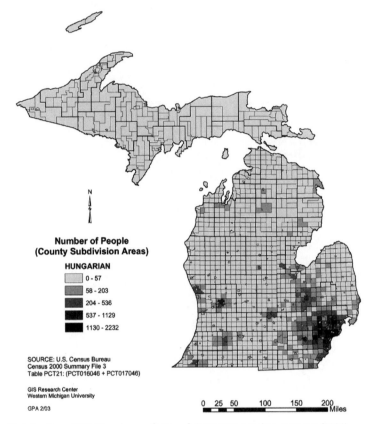

Distribution of Michigan's population claiming Hungarian ancestry (2000).

pendular migrants—that is, until the enactment of the severe immigration laws of 1924 made it impossible for them to continue to travel back and forth across the ocean time and again (see Appendix 1). Most immigrants, however, remained in the United States, became citizens, and formed Hungarian American communities where they welcomed, with varying degrees of enthusiasm, subsequent waves of their fellow country folk. Most of the following groups of Hungarian newcomers hailed from urban backgrounds and left their homeland for different reasons than had their rural predecessors, and they subsequently formed dissimilar relationships both with the American host population and with their natal land. The following is *a* story—but certainly not *the* story—of Hungarian Americans in Michigan.

Who Are the Magyars?

Magyar, or Magyarok (pl.), is the name Hungarians[2] use for themselves. The word "Hungarian" is derived from the word "Onogur," a Bulgarian-Turkish tribe's self-name. Between the sixth and eight centuries A.D. both the Hungarian tribes and the Onogurs were living just northeast of the Black Sea. They were in contact with one another, and when the Onogurs moved away, the Hungarians stayed and were called Hungarians. It is believed that the original Magyar tribes were an estimated 250,000 individuals who migrated from Asia and arrived in the Carpathian Basin of east-central Europe in the late ninth century. These tribes settled down, and with a blood oath promised to protect one another from outsiders and to stay on the land. Consequently, these tribes shifted from a nomadic and seminomadic pastoralist mode of subsistence to a sedentary and agriculturalist mode. Under their first king, István (who was later canonized and is often referred to as Szent István, meaning Saint Stephen), Hungarians accepted Christianity in 1001, a process that sounds much more peaceful than it must have been in reality.

The Carpathian Basin is a crossroad between East and West, and the Magyars were not welcome. As a result, their history is one of continued struggle with invaders and residents alike. A millennium after

Hungary

Hungary is situated between the northern latitudes of 45°48' and 48°35' and the eastern latitudes of 16°05' and 22°58'.

Covering an area of 35,934 square miles (93,030 square kilometers), the country is situated within the Carpathian Basin and is surrounded by the Carpathian Mountains, the Alps, and the Dinaric Alps. Hungary's total border length is 1,393 miles (2,242 kilometers). Of this, 221 miles (356 kilometers) are shared with Austria; 392 miles (631 kilometers) with the successor states of the former Yugoslavia (Yugoslavia, Croatia, and Slovenia); 268 miles (432 kilometers) with Romania; 134 miles (215 kilometers) with Ukraine; and 378 miles (608 kilometers) with Slovakia. The country has four distinct seasons and it lies in the temperate zone; the mean annual temperature is 50 degrees Fahrenheit (10 degrees Celsius). In the coldest month, January, it is the mean temperature is 34.1 degrees Fahrenheit (1.2 degrees Celsius), and in the warmest month, July, it is 71 degrees Fahrenheit (21.7 degrees Celsius). The Danube River divides Hungary. It is Europe's second-largest waterway after the Volga, and of its total length of 1,777 miles (2,860 kilometers), 259 miles (417 kilometers) are within Hungary. The capital, Budapest, is approximately in the center of the country and is bifurcated by the Danube River. The country has six major geographic areas: (1) the Great Hungarian Plain (Alföld); (2) the Western Lowland (Kis Alföld); (3) the Transdanubian Hills (Dunántúli Dombság); (4) the Central Mountain Range of Transdanubia (Dunántúli Középhegység); (5) the West Hungarian Border Region (Nyugat Magyar Peremvidék); and (6) the Northern Hills (Északi Középhegység).

their arrival in Central Europe, nineteenth-century Czech historian Frantisek Palacký—who was neither the first, the last, nor the only one to express disdain regarding Hungarians—wrote that the arrival of the Magyars in the Carpathian Basin was the greatest tragedy that had ever befallen the Slavs. Partially because of the strategic location of the Carpathian Basin, where they settled, the history of the Magyars is most turbulent, filled with invasions, wars, and occupations, resulting in a national self-image of isolation, martyrdom, and suffering as a bulwark of Western Christianity and civilization.[3]

This image is an apt one if we consider that the Tartar invasion in 1241 killed more than half of the Hungarian population. Other nationality groups had to be brought in and given land privileges if they were to populate the emptied settlements. The subsequent Ottoman occupation, which lasted for 150 years, was followed by centuries of Habsburg rule.

Hungary is a landlocked country in the center of Europe. There are some variations in culture and customs among its people that are related to environmental differences, though as a result of mass communication, travel, education, and a number of other factors, a great uniformity of culture is increasingly evident.

Since the early 1980s, Hungary has been experiencing a serious population decline. According to the Central Statistical Office (CSO), the country's population was 10,065,000 at the end of June 1999, 48,000 less than a year earlier. The CSO report shows that the number of marriages and births also fell, while the number of deaths increased compared to the same period in the previous year.

A Language out of Place

When the Magyars arrived in Central Europe, they had a complex tribal social organization and, most importantly, a clearly distinct linguistic and cultural identity. While hundreds of loan words entered the Hungarian language, and many cultural elements blended with those of their neighbors, the Magyar language remains distinctive. Unlike the languages spoken by the peoples of neighboring countries, Hungarian is a non-Indo-European language. It belongs to the Ugor branch of the Finno-Ugric family of languages. Its nearest linguistic relatives are the languages of the small Ostyak and Vogul tribes near the Ob River in Siberia. Finnish and Estonian are also related to the Hungarian language, but none of these languages are mutually understandable to their speakers.

In spite of very well developed regional identities, linguistic differences are small among Hungarian speakers. At the same time, however, a speaker can be easily categorized based on pronunciation and region-specific words and phrases. Thus, for example, speech identifies a person as a native of the eastern part of Hungary (the Great Hungarian Plain), of the western part of the country (Transdanubia), of its upper lands, or of the Széklerland in Transylvania, which was ceded to Romania in 1920.

Ethnic Diversity in Hungary

While approximately 97 percent of the population of present day Hungary is ethnic Hungarian whose mother tongue is Hungarian, the citizens of that country also include the following minorities: Armenians; Bulgarians; Croats; Germans; Greeks; Poles; Romanians; Roma (Gypsy); Ruthenians; Serbs; Slovaks; Slovenes; and Ukrainians. The largest minority group is the Roma (Gypsy), composing a very roughly estimated 6 percent of the country's population and numbering approximately 600,000. The Hungarian Roma are divided into several subgroups. There are about 170,000 ethnic Germans in Hungary. The Potsdam Treaty of 1948 resulted in the expulsion of 200,000 Germans from the country. The situation is similar with ethnic Slovaks, who number only 80,000 to 110,000 as a result of the joint population exchange between Hungary and (then) Czechoslovakia shortly after the Second World War. Smaller ethnic communities include about 35,000 Croatians, 5,000 Serbs, and 15,000 to 25,000 Romanians.

Before the Second World War, German was the most important and frequently used foreign language in Hungary. During the socialist period, Russian was a mandatory subject in schools and universities, though it never really became popular. Since the late 1980s, English has become the most valued foreign language in the country, particularly for younger Hungarians with ambitions in academia, the sciences, and business.

The most significant sign of Hungarian national identity is the linguistic and cultural connection that ties together the country's language, history, literature, music, folk culture, folk literature, and folk traditions.[4] Hungarians also include within their community ethnic Hungarians who live outside the present day boundaries of the country. At the same time, many ethnic Hungarians exclude members of the largest minority group, the Roma, a group whose members continuously struggle against great economic and social disadvantage.

In addition, there is a deep, almost permeating, consciousness that is yet another integral, and often perceptible, element of Hungarian national identity. It can be summarized as "we are all alone." It is based in part on often well-founded historical reasons, and on the "otherness" of the language and the origins (whether real or perceived) of the Hungarians amid their neighbors.

The Magyar or Hungarian language is spoken by a total of about fifteen million people worldwide. There are about thirteen million indigenous speakers in the Carpathian Basin. Over ten million Magyar speakers live within the present borders of Hungary, where 98 percent of the population speaks the language. More than two million Magyar speakers live in and are citizens of Romania, about six hundred thousand in Slovakia, three hundred thousand in the former Yugoslavia, almost two hundred thousand in Ukraine, and a couple thousand in Austria. The fact that over three million ethnic Hungarians live in neighboring countries means that Hungarians are one of the largest ethnic groups in contemporary Europe that lives outside its own homeland. Consequently, some scholars call Hungarians the "exiles of twentieth-century European history."[5]

The Trianon Treaty (1920) and Its Lasting Consequences

Extra Hungariam non est vita, et si est, non est ita
(Outside Hungary there is no life, and if there is life, it is
not like there).

"History weighs heavily on the Hungarian soul." Nobody can sum up the Hungarians' feelings about their fate as succinctly as did Martha Lampland in this single and bold sentence. Primarily for historical reasons, it is difficult to define who is a Hungarian and who is a Hungarian American. Complicating the issue of defining the latter is the fact that in the United States language is not necessarily a criterion for national or ethnic membership. This is clearly illustrated by the major difference between the number of individuals who state that by ancestry they are Hungarian (according to the 1990 United States Census, 997,545, with 110,337 of these foreign-born immigrants themselves) and those individuals over the age of five who speak Hungarian at home (147,902). While this does not necessarily mean that that there are fewer than 150,000 Hungarian speakers in the United States, it clearly shows that individuals consider themselves Hungarian who themselves or whose ancestors (even from several generations ago) came either from present-day Hungary or from anywhere within the Carpathian Basin (that is, areas that were parts of Hungary prior to the Trianon Treaty).

As a result of the Peace Treaty at Trianon in 1920,[6] two-thirds of Hungary's territory and 60 percent of its original population were ceded to Romania, Austria, Yugoslavia, and Czechoslovakia. This further complicates the definition of who is a Hungarian and who is a Hungarian American. Since the 1920s, individuals who identify themselves as ethnic Hungarians often have arrived in the United States from and as citizens of Austria, Romania, the Republic of Ukraine, and (after the 1991 separation of what was formerly known as Czechoslovakia) the Republic of Slovakia, as well as from the former Yugoslavia. At the time of their arrival, they are registered according to their citizenship and the country from which they hail and not according to their self-ascribed ethnic identity. Therefore, census data are not much help in estimating the number of ethnic Magyars anywhere in the world, including, of course, the United States in general and Michigan in particular.

Hungarians Coming to America

There are intriguing legends about Hungarians among the crew of Leif Eriksson in the year 1000; as well as among the first people who greeted Christopher Columbus when he accidentally found himself on our shores.[7] Legend also has it that Hungarians participated in a sixteenth-century colonizing voyage that was directed by Queen Elizabeth of England. There are actual records of a Hungarian colonel in the army of George Washington who was one of 141 Hungarian soldiers distinguishing themselves in the American Revolution. Many Hungarian soldiers fought in the American Civil War. Stories exist about Sándor Bölöni Farkas, who visited North America in 1831 and subsequently published his vivid impressions, which undoubtedly influenced some of his countrymen to try their fortunes in the United States. However, until the last third of the nineteenth century there was little or no substantial emigration from Hungary, or rather, as it was known between 1867 and the First World War, the Austro-Hungarian Dual Monarchy.[8]

Six Waves of Immigrants from Hungary

H ungarian immigration dates back to the middle 1800s because until the middle of the nineteenth century a feudal system prevailed in Hungary, so the majority of its peasantry was downtrodden and place-bound. Therefore, there was no appreciable mass emigration until sometime after the de jure collapse of the feudal order in 1848. Indeed, with the exception of wartime dislocations, postwar resettlements, and relocations during Hungary's history, until the 1860s there was very little voluntary mass emigration beyond Hungary's national borders.

Michigan has been host to six different waves of emigration from Hungary between the 1880s and the early 2000s. Even though, as we will see, there are some similarities between these waves, they occurred in rather different social and political contexts. That is, the push and pull factors, the processes and rates of emigration, the destination of emigrants, their educational levels and social backgrounds, as well as their ability and desire to adapt to the ways of the host society were markedly different from one phase to the next. There were also variations between these groups' relationships with and expectations of their homeland and their natal culture, and in the creation of, adherence to, and strategies of immigrant associations and organizations.

The First Wave: The Changing Functions of the Church

> . . . rally to the work of [the] church [because] the church is the pro-
> tector of the community, . . . the conserver of the values of the past,
> creator of ideals in the present and the torchbearer of tomorrow's
> progress. . . . The church is the great mother of the young . . . educat-
> ing them . . . preparing them to meet the moral demands of the
> world. . . .
>
> —Tibor Tóth, Historical Album for the Dedication of the Hungarian Reformed Church, 1941

The first and largest wave of Hungarian immigration took place in the
period between the 1880s and the First World War, when an estimated
1,893,647 immigrants arrived from within Hungary's borders. The primary push factor was tremendous poverty and hopelessness. This was
also a period of heavy industrialization in the United States, so the pull
factors were particularly powerful. In 1907, the peak year of immigration, 193,460 people arrived from Hungary—an astonishing 15 percent
of the year's total immigrants of 1,285,439. It is difficult to determine,
however, how many of these immigrants were ethnic Hungarians and
how many could be classified as ethnic Romanians, Serbians, Slovaks,
Ruthenians, Germans, or as belonging to other nationality groups who
lived within the borders of greater Hungary. However, we know that, as
parts of chain migrations, many came alone, many more men than
women came, and nearly 70 percent of these immigrants were farm-
hands or farmers. The remaining were primarily unskilled workers, factory hands, miners, or domestic servants. Indeed, most of the
immigrants in this first wave were poor peasants, who had barely eked
out a living in the Austro-Hungarian Monarchy.[9] As one of Hungary's
most outstanding poets, Attila József, lamented in a poem he titled *My
Homeland*, "a million and a half staggered out [of their homeland]."
These emigrants left their remote rural villages for economic reasons
(see Appendix 1). Their main intentions were to become miners or factory or agrarian workers in the United States, to make and save as much
money in as short a period of time as possible, and, with their savings,
to return to their villages and resume their rural lifestyles. Therefore,
most of these immigrants remained transients. Paradoxically, this was

initially true even for those early Magyar immigrants, who, for political or personal reasons after the Treaty of Trianon was implemented, found themselves without a homeland and ended up staying in the States. They had no desire or motivation to learn English or to leave their various immigrant enclaves other than to go to work in their factories or mines, where they found themselves laboring among immigrants of many different nationalities.

The primary associations around which these early immigrants rallied were churches, boardinghouses, and social insurance organizations. The function of immigrant churches changed quite radically from that of churches in the homeland. In the United States, churches became worldlier and more social, with each church having a "halle," or great hall, where the various church suppers, fund-raising events, and social and other secular gatherings could be held.

While it is impossible to determine for certain the extent of circular or return migration in this or any of the later waves of immigration, scholars estimate that between 16 and 25 percent of this group eventually returned to their homeland either permanently or temporarily.[10] There were "professional immigrants" during this period, individuals who crossed the ocean six or more times in a regular pattern of what I call pendular or circular migration (see Appendix 2).

The first groups of Hungarians arrived in southeastern Michigan in the late 1880s—they were attracted by the job opportunities in factories, foundries, and manufacturing plants during a particularly brisk industrial boom in the region. Significantly, Detroit was a place of secondary settlement for many of these immigrants, the majority of whom were men. Originally from small and economically disadvantaged rural villages in Hungary, they first tried their luck with farm work in the United States and Canada, or worked in mines in West Virginia, Kentucky, Pennsylvania, and the Upper Peninsula of Michigan. Some of them left factory jobs in Ohio, Illinois, and Indiana because they had heard about higher wages and better working conditions in Michigan. In other cases, as a number of informants recalled, a *koma*—a fellow villager—beckoned: "Hey, join us here: In Detroit even the fences are woven of sausage!" or "Come, five of us are already here from your village of birth, Sarud, work and live with us."[11]

Delray

The primary locus of Hungarian settlement in southeastern Michigan was Delray. This independent village was formed in the late 1800s from what was previously known as a section of Fort Dearborn. According to informants and contemporary documents and photographs alike, Delray was a pleasant, fairly prosperous, and quiet community, even after it was annexed to Detroit in 1904.[12] From the various sources one gets a rather idyllic image of early American industrial life in Delray: flowers and gardens everywhere; cow pastures alongside foundries, factories, and manufacturing plants; and chickens pecking near nicely paved streets under fancy street lights (see Appendix 1). In-migration of large numbers of Hungarians to Michigan really began in earnest in 1898, the year in which the Michigan Malleable Iron Company began production in Delray.

In 1904 this rural-residential yet heavily industrial and urbanizing village five miles from the very center of Detroit's downtown was annexed to the city—despite the angry protests of Delray residents. At that time thirty Hungarian families already owned property in Delray.[13] There was also one Hungarian saloon, operating since 1901, which served multiple social, economic, and cultural functions. As the widow of its original proprietor recalled,

> There was no center for the Hungarians of Delray. Our saloon was everything, all in one. . . . We did all kinds of business besides selling liquor. We made the place home-like and lots of single men ate in our saloon. We had a kind of bank too. . . . The people brought us their money to deposit for them. We remitted money to Europe. . . . We sold steamship tickets and real estate. If the people wanted to have a meeting, they held it in the hall above our saloon. We conducted a sort of general merchandise store right there also.[14]

Lucrative work in automobile factories attracted thousands more Hungarians to the area after 1910.[15] By the eve of the First World War, the Delray section of Detroit was known in popular parlance and by the media as "Little Hungary," "Little Budapest," or "Hunkytown." The rapid

Steve Szabo, owner of Szabo's Meat Market and Delicatessen in Delray, Michigan (photo courtesy of Éva V. Huseby-Darvas).

influx of Hungarians had essentially displaced most of the Armenians and Poles from the center of the Delray section to its peripheries. Thus there was a marked and identifiable geographic separation of the three major ethnic groups in the relatively small settlement.[16]

Regardless of ethnic affiliation, however, most Delray residents worked together in one of the local factories, foundries, or plants. While they often worked side by side for twelve to fourteen hours each workday, verbal communication between Hungarian and other laborers was limited because of the lack of a common language. Learning English was not considered to be important, old informants said, since most of the Delray Hungarians were planning to stay in America just long enough to save enough money to return to their villages, buy some land, or pay the back taxes, and resume their traditional rural lives.

During this phase, a large number of Delray Hungarians were either single men or married men whose families remained in Hungary. Many lived like guest workers, maintaining a transient lifestyle. Some of them made the journey to America a number of times, and considered their American experiences as harsh but temporary phases of their lives, driven by economic necessity. They lived in boardinghouses, or as they called it, *burdosházak*, among their "own kind," saved as much of their income as they could, and concentrated all their energies on going back home.

Delray's development was typical of many other Hungarian American settlements in the rapidly industrializing regions of the United States.[17] The first decade or so of the Delray Hungarian colony may best be characterized as an urban-nomadic phase. Formal social organizations (such as the local mutual benefit associations, social and cultural clubs, and religious and secular formations) established themselves rapidly, existed briefly, and disappeared without much trace. Membership in nationally organized churches and mutual benefit societies (such as the Roman Catholic, Byzantine-rite Catholic, and Reformed Churches and the Verhovay—later William Penn—and Kossuth Societies) turned over rapidly. In 1910 the majority of the approximately eight thousand Hungarians who lived in the Detroit area inhabited and worked in the densely populated Delray section.[18] They constituted a community in the geographic sense of the term, and formed a fragmented and rather loosely knit social community as well. In that early phase, however, these Hungarians did not forge a symbolic community; a common shared consciousness, or a sense of belonging together—in other words, ethnic solidarity—was just not there. As we will see in the following section, the First World War radically changed this situation, so that by 1930 the city of Detroit had a Hungarian population of 22,311 and was the fourth-largest center of Hungarian settlement in the United States (after New York, Cleveland, and Chicago).[19] At this time it became a real immigrant community.

Immigrants between the Two World Wars

The second major group of Hungarians came to the United States between the two World Wars, when about thirty thousand individuals arrived from the Carpathian Basin. This was a much smaller wave than the first because in the early 1920s new and restrictive American immigration laws blocked the way of potential newcomers. From 1929 the Great Depression further reduced the chances and numbers of immigrants. During this period there were also return migrations of Hungarian Americans who returned from Hungary directly to the States if they were already American citizens, or, if they were not, came indirectly and clandestinely through Canada.[20]

However, a significant percentage of newcomers during the interwar period came from the urban middle classes and left their homeland for political rather than economic reasons. World War I and its consequences, the painful implementation of the Trianon Treaty, foreign army occupations, and a couple of unsuccessful but bloody revolutions were the major upheavals of this period that gave more than enough political reasons for many to become either persecuted, self-exiled, or banished from Hungary. Many were highly educated professionals; quite a few came from urban Jewish families. A number of these immigrants became internationally known in their various fields. Among these "illustrious immigrants," as Laura Fermi calls them, are Theodore von Kármán in the field of aeronautics[21]; Paul Erdős in mathmatics; John von Neumann in the mathematical theory of games and the development of missiles and computers; Leó Szilárd, Edward Teller, and Eugene Wígner in the field of physics, particularly relating to nuclear energy; György von Békésy and Albert Szent-Györgyi in medicine and physiology; Béla Bartók, Eugene Ormándy, Fritz Reiner, György Solti, József Szigeti, and György Széll, among numerous others, in music; Ferenc Molnár and Kate Serédy in literature; and too many to mention in the entertainment industry in general and Hollywood in particular. I will return to this topic later in a brief section on the contributions of Hungarian Americans. Unlike their predecessors, who wanted to and at times did indeed return home, for these politically motivated émigrés, returning to the homeland was rarely an issue. While a few of these newcomers joined earlier established associations, many started their own social insurance organizations, churches, burial societies, and particularly political associations, and formed both formal and informal cultural institutions.

In the Detroit area, as in other immigrant enclaves, this was the time of the crystallization of the Hungarian American community. At this time the Hungarian ethnic radio and press began to flourish, as did amateur plays, poetry and prose readings, church and cultural center suppers, dances, and such. The lobbying of some of these émigrés, particularly for the return of territories and populations lost at the Treaty of Trianon, was evident in many of their publications and in the immigrant and national media.[22] The churches, with their formal and informal groups and social networks, were instrumental in the economic survival of the entire community during the Great Depression.

Starting an ethnic radio program was a very important process for the Hungarian American community in the period between the two World Wars and beyond. Instrumental in this process was Ernő Pálos. An émigré newcomer, Pálos was born in Pancsova (part of pre-Trianon Treaty Hungary), the second son of a moderately affluent secular Jewish family. He became a journalist and moved to Budapest. After the First World War and the tremendous political turmoil that followed, Pálos, like so many others, left Hungary, and went to stay with his brother, who practiced medicine in Cleveland. After meeting, courting, and marrying a young woman who was born in Detroit of Hungarian American parents and—as she told me—at the time of their marriage did not speak more than a few words Hungarian, Mr. Pálos moved to Michigan in the early 1930s. Thus for him, like for so many others before and since, Michigan became a place of secondary settlement in North America.

Mr. Pálos was already the publisher of the local weekly paper, the *Detroiti Magyarság*—Detroit Hungarians—when on 19 January 1936 he started a new venture, a radio program, the Hungarian Rhapsody Hour. At first, Mr. Pálos broadcast live music and skits, performed by amateur actors and actresses, musicians and vocalists, Gypsy orchestras, and chamber music groups, as well as children's recitals. Most of the performers were members of the huge and, apparently in spite of the Great Depression, still growing local Hungarian community. Initially a five-minute hygiene program by Delray physician Miklós Gáldonyi, along with numerous advertisements from local and regional merchants and services, were also included in the hourly programs each week.

However, as his widow Margaret told me in the fluent Hungarian that Mr. Pálos taught her when she was in her midtwenties, by the late 1930s prerecorded entertainment was the dominant mode, interspersed with occasional live acts for special occasions, like anniversary and holiday programs. In addition to the Sunday hour, a thirty-minute program each Saturday on the same station was devoted to amateur shows performed by children of the community. As I was told directly by numerous people who remembered these early years of the Hungarian radio programs from Delray and far beyond, this forum was tremendously significant in stimulating the enthusiastic upkeep and cultivation of the language, music, and other elements of Hungarian culture.

As Mrs. Pálos recalled, "World War II transformed the program. During the war years the Saturday broadcast was used exclusively for the reading of letters sent by our soldiers from overseas."

The Sunday hour was used by Ernő Pálos as the primary vehicle for a number of successful war bond and Red Cross fund-raising drives, which were, according to his widow, widely emulated by other immigrant groups. As a result of these drives the local Hungarian community received several honorable citations. "Thus," Mrs. Pálos said, "our people did not suffer as much as they did during the first war around here from prejudice stemming from Hungary's enemy nation status. Even though the programs were allowed to function uninterruptedly throughout the war years, an English-language transcript of the program was required and examined by the War Department prior to each broadcast."

In 1952, when Ernő Pálos died, his widow took over as newspaper publisher and as radio-program manager, hostess, and announcer. Financial and other problems made it impossible to maintain all as it had been: first the Saturday children's half hour was lost, "mainly," Mrs. Pálos told me, "because radio stations toss and shove around programs catering to smaller national groups in favor of larger listening audiences. . . . It is more profitable . . . when they sell more ads." Then, in the late 1970s, Mrs. Pálos was forced to sell the newspaper. Yet, as she maintained during one of our conversations in the early 1980s, "the Sunday radio program must go on as it has since 1936. . . . The audience wants, needs, and appreciates it as it is and as it has been since its inception."[23]

Delray, the small area in downriver Detroit, remained for many decades the most important focus of Hungarian life, not only in southeast Michigan but also beyond, as Zoltán Veres[24] so fondly recalled:

> Delray, a compact Hungarian residential/business/entertainment center (which has developed under the shadow of the factories that provided jobs for eager working families), was a magnet for Windsorites, who crossed over to Detroit by bridge, ferry-boat and tunnel, to visit relatives, to attend churches or church-functions, to dine and dance at favorite hot-spots (Ne Tovább, Kovács Bár, Hungarian Village and so many others) to the beat of Gypsy orchestras (János Brenkács, Ziggy Béla), to buy imported foods from Hungary (preserves, paprika from Szeged, salamis, etc.) and of course to attend the movie theatre which featured Hungarian film stars such as Jávor Pál, Kabos Gyula. . . . On Sunday afternoons, Windsorites flocked to Detroit to catch the latest . . . film. Hungarian radio . . . connected Detroit and Windsor and ensured that Hungarians were up-to-snuff on popular tunes and upcoming events. Today Hungarian Radio (on WNZK) continues that tradition. . . . (Zoltán Veres, personal communication in 2002)

The Trauma of "DPs"

The third phase of Hungarian immigration occurred between the end of World War II and the middle of the 1950s, during which time an estimated twenty-five thousand Hungarians entered the United States under the Displaced Persons Act, becoming known as "DPs," after the initial letters of the act. Similar to those who entered the country between the two World Wars, most DPs were urban and highly educated. They also left the homeland mainly for political reasons: to escape from communism and Soviet domination.[25] Some of the DPs were members of the Hungarian Christian middle class. Others hailed from well-known upper-, middle-aristocratic, or lesser-gentry backgrounds. Many were prominent and high-ranking officers in Hungary's army. Still others were Jews or Roma who left Europe after they somehow survived the German occupation and the Holocaust under which the majority of their relatives and friends had perished. Some of the DPs came from Hungary proper, while others arrived from territories ceded in the Trianon Treaty. For whatever reason, many DPs experienced tremendous trauma before their arrival in the United States, which was often followed, once they settled down, by a radical and painful socioeconomic fall. Hungarian degrees and professions—particularly in medicine, law, politics, army carriers, and teaching—were neither accepted nor often applicable in the United States. High-ranking army officers thus became unskilled factory workers in automobile and other manufacturing plants. It is not surprising that many of these immigrants, who were already highly politicized and ideologized upon their arrival, created, articulated, and perpetuated a particular, mostly interwar Hungarian identity and passionate and often bitter nationalism. There are scholars who maintain that these identities and affinities are no longer viable or timely, and, understandably, the DPs often find themselves far from their motherland's contemporary reality.[26] In Hungarian American associations some of these individuals have locked themselves into what György Csepeli called during a conversation "a mirrored labyrinth," in which they reinforce each other's Hungarianness and recognize actual, imagined, or alleged pre–World War II titles and ranks that are no longer recognized by anyone else. Mostly for political reasons, and occasionally for personal ones, many DPs did not return to Hungary even for visits until the late 1980s or early 1990s, if at all, and therefore it is understandable that, after more than a half a century of immigrant life, their particular Hungarianness is atavistic and their image of Hungarian reality has long ceased to reflect the actuality of their homeland. The immigrant associations formed by members of this wave of immigration are perhaps the most complex among all their counterparts. These include the World Federation of Hungarian Veterans and some branches of the Hungarian Scout Association Exterris. In the mid-1990s these organizations were not only still operating—in spite of their aging membership—but also appeared to be well functioning, providing their members both the very reason for their being and the motivation for not returning permanently to their homeland after the end of communism (that is, after the cessation of the very reason for which many of the DPs originally left Hungary).

The "'56ers"

The fourth phase of immigration from Hungary was constituted mainly of the so-called '56ers, individuals who left Hungary after the 1956 Hungarian Revolution. Many members of this immigrant wave were young, single, urban, and moderately or well–educated; some were even accomplished in their fields. Among all the groups of Magyar immigrants, the '56ers were the most warmly welcomed, both by the host society and (at least initially, until realization of major differences in values and worldviews) also by members of earlier immigrant groups, most of whom were joyous about and identified with (though often misinterpreted) the Hungarian Revolution of 1956. The '56ers were readily helped by the host society, primarily because of their status as actual—or purported—freedom fighters against communism in the atmosphere of cold war and the overall political and economic situation in the United States at the time of their arrival. Many '56ers were—and remain—highly politicized and ideologized, and were actively involved in movements regarding their homeland. Some scholars suggest that this group's politics, lobbying, and other strategies, as well as their relations with the homeland, are somewhat less archaic and a bit more pragmatic than those of many of the DPs.[27] The reason that '56ers hold a somewhat more realistic image of the homeland than the DPs is that many '56ers began paying regular visits to Hungary after they received political amnesty there in 1963. Thus, they have had an intensive relationship with their homeland. Nevertheless, after a while living away from the homeland, in a sense time stands still for all immigrants. The homeland becomes a symbol and an abstraction, rather than a concrete place. The lobbying of the '56ers—through such organizations as the Hungarian Freedom Fighters Federation, the Hungarian Human Rights Foundation, the World Federation of Hungarians, the Hungarian Lobby, and others—is evident in the daily national and local media and in the widely circulated letters and petitions addressed to the president of the United States and to Washington, D.C., circles, as well as in lively, frequently heated discussions on electronic mail networks.

A '56er with the Statue of Liberty in the background (photograph courtesy of Robert M. Darvas).

Kádár's Orphans

The fifth wave of immigrants from Hungary could be called "Kádár's orphans." Individuals who were unhappy with the politics and regime of János Kádár, which was based on the notion of "those who are not against us are with us," escaped from Hungary during that regime and came to the United States between the 1960s and the late 1980s. Some of these individuals left their homeland because they did not like the political regime; others left for a combination of economic, political, and familial reasons. All, regardless of the reason for their emigration, worked diligently to establish themselves in the United States. Interestingly, some of these individuals appear to be less involved with the larger economic and political issues relating to their homeland than are the DPs and the '56ers. At the same time, "Kádár's orphans" maintain what appear to be considerably more intensive relations with friends and family in the homeland, with many more visits to Hungary and to relatives residing there than are typical of members of the other immigrant groups.

"New Blood"? Post-1989 Immigrants

The sixth (and still ongoing) phase of Hungarian immigration is com-
prised of ethnic Hungarians who left their homelands after 1989, after
the demise of socialism and for many the beginning of a very trying
political, social, and economic period. During this time, Hungary—as
well as the entire so-called former Soviet Block—shifted from a command economy to the "call of the capitalist market," a harsh, costly, and
decidedly painful process for the bulk of Hungary's citizens. Interestingly, yet not surprisingly, just like those in the very first major wave a
century ago, the great majority of these newcomers have come to the
United States for mainly economic reasons, and many engage in a pendular migration similar to that common among members of the first
wave. In their homelands these immigrants did not see much hope for
themselves. In general, however they have had considerably higher and
more concrete expectations of the West than did immigrants before
them. As one individual from an earlier wave lamented: "these newcomers now know exactly what labels of clothes and other goods they
want."

Included in the last two waves of immigrants are those ethnic
Hungarians who came from Transylvania and left primarily for political
reasons—because as ethnic minorities they continued to be discrimi-
nated against—and thus have no desire to return permanently to their
homeland. Many of these individuals are very active in various chap-
ters of the American Transylvanian Federation. They formed and have
rigorously maintained a vital and vibrant organization, the Hungarian
Heritage Preservation Circle (Magyar Hagyományokat Ápoló Kör).
Organized in 1990, the Circle is part of the Hungarian Reformed Church
in Allen Park, Michigan, where members of the Circle meet regularly,
with formal gatherings held on the second Sunday of each month.
These gatherings are one of the very few places where Hungarian and
only Hungarian is spoken; at most other meetings and functions, more
and more English is used. Yet, in general, members of this group stay at
a certain distance from most other Hungarian American associations.
Like most newcomers, they focus their everyday activities on trying to
make an economic go of it in the United States, a host country that,

The Stated Aim of the Hungarian Heritage Preservation Circle

The publication of the Hungarian Heritage Preservation Circle states the identity of the members and the goals of the organization, and reads as follow:

> We are Hungarian Americans in Detroit area who lived unforgettable periods of their lives in the Old Country, in Central Europe. We have been challenged to face special responsibilities through our lifestories. While establishing new life in our new country, the United States of America, we have remained tied with unbreakable cultural, emotional, and family ties to the Old Country. While being proud American citizens, our Hungarian identity remains an unforgettable part of our lives. Living this dual challenge, we felt it necessary to launch a community that can help our special problems.

The goal of the circle:

> Our goal and responsibility is to preserve what we brought with us, and enrich ourselves and others. It is very important for us to keep the Hungarian heritage alive among the second and third generation Hungarian Americans, and inspire them to understand European History and Culture [*sic*]. Our preserving the Hungarian heritage does not come from a negative attitude toward our new country. On the contrary, we are thankful for everything we have received from America. *As a matter of fact, it is this country that has given a chance to many of us to freely and openly live out our Hungarian identity.* As proud American citizens we would like to provide a community for all of those for whom the Hungarian heritage means responsibility and an enriching spiritual source. [Emphasis mine. Publication provided kind courtesy of Mrs. Györgyi Míkó].

particularly in the late 1990s and early 2000s, offers fewer opportunities than these immigrants had initially hoped. The strain in the relationship between the last two groups of immigrants and the earlier waves is particularly evident in contemporary Hungarian American associational life, which, contrary to expectations of scholars and members of older associations alike, these newcomers have failed to revitalize.

Moreover, the political activities of many members of the last two waves are different from those of previous groups. In some cases these activities don't seem to exist: the newcomers are involved with establishing themselves, with making a living, and with establishing a future for their children. Their focus is on the domestic rather than the public or political sphere. In other cases, and these seem to be the majority, the political activities of these immigrants are limited to charitable contributions and supporting specific institutions, such as churches, orphanages, schools, colleges, universities, or old folks homes in their homeland. In still other cases, however, some newcomers are intensively involved with the political, social, and cultural problems of their natal land, and this involvement seems to be expressed primarily on the Internet, in fervent political discussions among those who comprise the latest wave of the brain-drain.

Demographic Profile of Hungarian Americans in Michigan

While for reasons discussed in the previous sections it is difficult to state with certainty how many Hungarian Americans there are, and exactly what their socioeconomic circumstances are, let me attempt to make some generalizations with the help of the 1990 United States Census. The data about the Hungarian American population mirror both the homeland's aging population and the dismal reproduction rate in Hungary (though during the first couple of decades of the twentieth century, fecundity among immigrant women from Hungary was more than twice that of native-born Hungarians). From the census data we can ascertain that—including both the so-called natives, who were born in the United States but identify themselves as Hungarians by one or more ancestor, and those who were born in Hungary or in neighboring countries—the approximately 997,545 Hungarian Americans live in 446,741 households. While there are Hungarian Americans in all fifty states, the ten states that they most favor are: Ohio, New York, California, Pennsylvania, New Jersey, Michigan, Florida, Illinois, Connecticut, and Indiana, as shown in Table 1. The 2000 Census estimated that there were 118,651 people of Hungarian ancestry in Michigan at that time.

Table 1. Hungarian Population in Selected States

STATE	NUMBER OF HUNGARIAN AMERICANS	PERCENTAGE OF ALL HUNGARIAN AMERICANS
Ohio	144,002	14.44
New York	115,981	11.63
California	104,722	10.50
Pennsylvania	92,006	9.22
New Jersey	88,361	8.86
Michigan	71,135	7.13
Florida	68,049	6.82
Illinois	40,232	4.03
Connecticut	31,631	3.17
Indiana	26,548	2.66

Small households, with one or two individuals, dominate: 27 percent of the natives and 32.6 percent of the foreign-born Hungarians live in single-person households, while 35.2 percent of the natives and 35.6 percent of the foreign-born live in two-person households. Thus the average household size is small, with 2.34 persons per household among the native population, and 1.70 persons among the foreign-born population. The median age of the native-born Hungarian Americans is 37.1 years, while that of their foreign-born counterparts is 56.6 years.

Even though marriage data do not tell us who marries whom, it is well known from other sources that, particularly since the 1960s, the role of nationality in the immigrants' and their children's selection of spouses is weakening. The 1990 census data illustrate that most adult Hungarian Americans are married, and fertility data show that the rate of fecundity, as in the homeland, is very low. For individuals over the age of fifteen among the foreign-born, 73 percent of the men and 54.4 percent of the women are married, while among their native cohorts 62.4 percent of the men and 54.8 percent of the women are married. Cohabitation in unmarried partnerships appears to be rare: 1.4 percent of the native-born, and less than 1 percent (0.94 percent) of the foreign-born admitted to such an arrangement. The rate of divorce among the native men is 6.5 percent, and 9 percent among the women; and among the foreign-born men it is 8.6 percent, and 9 percent among the foreign-born women.

Women of childbearing age are defined by the census as those between the ages of fifteen and forty-four. Among the natives there are 997 children per 1,000 women in this cohort, while among the foreign-born there are 1,434 children per 1,000 women. Neither number reaches anywhere near the replacement or reproduction of the population. The majority of Hungarian American nuclear families with children under the age of eighteen appear to be "intact," if the data that among the foreign-born 86.1 percent and among the native-born 82.2 percent of children under the age of eighteen live in a household where both of their parents are present are a reliable indication of that. Among Hungarian Americans who are twenty-five years of age or older, 80.8 percent have completed high school (82.9 percent of the natives and 69.7 percent of the foreign-born), while 26.8 percent have attained at least a bachelor's degree from college or university (27.2 of the natives, 24.4 percent of the foreign-born).

The economic status of Hungarian Americans is reflected by the per capita and family median incomes. Among the native-born the 1989 per capita income was $19,883, while among the foreign-born it was $25,712. The family median income for the native-born was $42,714, and for the foreign-born this was $43,266. The family mean income for the native-born was $54,739, and for the foreign-born it was $59,076. While it appears from these figures that the foreign-born do considerably better financially than do the native-born, the individuals who live below poverty level, particularly those over the age of sixty-five, seem to contradict this. Among the native-born families 4.2 percent live below the poverty line, while among the foreign-born this figure is 4.9 percent; but among those native-born individuals who are sixty-five years of age or older, 13.1 percent live below poverty line, while 25.1 percent of their foreign-born cohorts do.

The unemployment rate among native-born individuals over the age of sixteen is 4.5 percent, while among their foreign-born cohorts it is 5.3 percent. It is difficult to determine an occupational pattern; however, the data show that more than one-fourth of Hungarian Americans work as professionals or in service-related industries. It is not easy to interpret what the overwhelmingly large category labeled "Not in the Labor Force" means: people in this category are retired, in school, working "only" in the household, and so on. Yet in the population over the age of sixteen among the native-born Hungarian Americans 38.8 percent of the total, and 43 percent of the women are in this category, while among their foreign cohorts 48.4 percent of the total, and 62.9 percent of the women are not in the labor force. Obviously we see here the work pattern of an aging and aged population, yet it is also possible that in part a traditionally much desired but very seldom realized pattern of husbands working and women staying home to maintain the household is reflected by these data.

Hungarian Ethnic Life in Michigan

How do contemporary Hungarian Americans in Michigan express their ethnicity? In the private or domestic sphere this is asserted with home decorations, photographs, artwork, certain carved furniture, and books focusing on Hungarian themes and in the Hungarian language. The most important and apparently lasting manner in which ethnicity is maintained through the generations, however, is through foodways. The expression of and emphases on Hungarian ethnicity through particular dishes are evident in both the private and public spheres. One very important way in which a number of people, mostly but not all women, manifest their Hungarianness is by gathering together and, in groups, making a particular type of egg noodles, selling these, and turning the profit over to their church.

Foodways of Hungarian Americans in Michigan

It might sound like a cliché, but food, a lavishly set table, and obvious abundance and variety are immensely important among Hungarian Americans, and are part of what is commonly referred to as "*the* genuine and proper Hungarian hospitality." It is the most natural thing for a hostess to offer (and keep offering!) food, coffee, and pastries, and for

Mariska Leleszi (standing) with the Roma players in the Hungarian American tent at the Michigan Folklife Festival, on the campus of Michigan State University, East Lansing, Michigan, 1988 (photo courtesy of Robert M. Darvas).

the host to offer drinks, whenever anyone enters a house. Hungarian Americans, like most ethnic groups, I imagine, are very proud of their national dishes. It seems that, even in the third, fourth, or later generations, when no other signs of Hungarianness remain, still present are specific ways of preparing and eating a certain dish, or a desire to find an authentic recipe for a certain dish, or at least a happy memory of a "real Hungarian dish," perhaps something that lingers on from one's childhood. Furthermore, contrary to some sticklers for "authenticity," it really does not seem to matter for most if that dish is "authentic" or not, as long as it has the power to evoke particular "ethnic memories" with its color, smell, flavor, consistency, or even just its name. This is illustrated by some of the conversations I had with people in the city of Flint and the areas surrounding it. As Rózsi Horváth, a DP and a resident of Burton, Michigan, told me,

> We lived in Delray between 1951 and 1957. Then, when I married a '56er
> . . . his sister was brought out in 1936 by her godmother . . . [so] we

moved here to be close to her. There were so many Hungarians here in
'56ers, churches, clubs, guilds, and of course *then* there were plenty of
jobs. . . . There was the St. Elizabeth [Women's] Society but it merged
with the St. Joseph Men's Society so today there is no longer a women's
group in the Blessed Sacrament Church. But we [the women] still
make *kolbász* and *hurka* [Hungarian sausages], and bake *kifli* and
kalács [crescent-cookies and sweet bread usually filled with poppy-
seeds and walnuts] for all the fund-raising events and before the holidays, and, yes, they sell really well. But this is a dying community. . . .
We had 160 people attending a recent Hungarian dance, but maybe
half were Hungarians, and many came from the downriver [Detroit]
area. . . . It is hard to tell who were the Hungarians. . . . I really don't
know how many Hungarians are still here. So many died in the last few
years, so I would say not too many of us are left. There are no youth
groups, but that is no wonder since there are very few young people
around here. Why would they come here and why would they stay?
Anymore there are mostly older folks in the Flint and Burton area.

A few days before her ninety-sixth birthday, I visited with Mrs. Kató
Puskás of Flint. She was born in 1895 in Ibrány, Szabolcs County, and,
after working as a domestic in New York for a few months, she arrived
in Flint in 1919 and never left. She recalled that

> There were *so* many Hungarians in Flint, my dear. Buick and General
> Motors brought the folks here. Like a fly to sweet honey, that was how
> it was then. So many came that some had to stay in tents. . . . Between
> 1920 and 1930 the young folks were so active, you should have seen.
> Most of the Hungarian churches were built then. Even after the war
> [World War II] many new ones came and they also liked it here. But
> only a few '56ers came here. Most did not stay long. Only about three
> or four '56er families stayed around, who knows why? Nobody treated
> them kinder than we did, but they still just left us . . . and, you see, any-
> more there are just a few of us old ones left here.

A young minister, the Reverend Péter Pál Bodor of the Hungarian
Reformed Church of Flint, was studying mechanical engineering when

I talked with him in the early 1990s. He had arrived in Flint in the mid-1980s from his native Transylvania, after finishing theology seminar in the city of Arad. The reverend observed that special kinds of foods, particular holidays, festivals, and Gypsy music were the primary attraction, and for some of his flock the only attraction:

> Many come to church only on particular days of the year, for example, December twenty-fifth and Easter Sunday. They only come, they tell me, because, their grandfathers used to go to church on that day too. They also come in droves for special foods. For example, they buy Hungarian *kolbász, kifli, kalács* because, they tell me, only their mothers, grandmothers, or grandfathers were able to make these taste like they taste here and Christmas or Easter or Whitsuntide would not be the same without these on their tables. Many also come to the annual . . . [dance] . . . this year it was held in the Burton Roman Catholic Church, and the Saint Joseph Club organized it. The attraction? They come because of the Hungarian stuffed cabbage, Hungarian *csirke paprikás* [chicken paprikas], the special noodles, the good, rich pastries, and of course the Gypsy band . . . for these the old Hungarians and their children and some grandchildren come. But remember that most of the Hungarian immigrants here are in their seventies and eighties. . . . Yes, there is a Hungarian women's group here, it used to be called "Zsuzsanna Lórántffy Women's Association," but today they simply call it the "Women's Guild," because the name did not mean anything anymore for most of the members.[28] The women volunteer their time and energy, the church buys all the ingredients and they cook and bake. Each time they make various kinds of Hungarian sausages, bake 1,200 dozen *kifli*, and 800 *kalács* for fund-raising. Every time they make several thousand dollars for the church with the sausages, and at least twice as much with the pastries.

In the following section I will discuss another food-related activity and a group, "the Wednesday Hungarians." They not only ate Hungarian meals on each Wednesday when they gathered at the Hungarian Reformed Church in Allen Park, Michigan, but also prepared many pounds of csiga noodles, a very small and labor-intensive pasta that is believed to be a uniquely Hungarian noodle.[29] Therefore it is not a surprise that many Hungarian Americans with whom I worked during various research projects in the Detroit area and elsewhere in southeastern Michigan consider the preparation of, purchase of, and feast on csiga noodles to be a specifically Hungarian custom and thus an integral part of their ethnic heritage and (sometimes second-, third-, even fourth-generation) ethnic identity.[30] The gathering and activity was most meaningful for the participants.[31]

Csiga Noodle Making among Hungarian Americans in Michigan

The noodle-making gatherings at the church that I studied regularly drew between forty and sixty older women and six to eight older men. By seven o'clock on an average Wednesday morning, the day when these regular weekly sessions took place, Mrs. Juliska Biró was at work preparing the basic noodle dough by hand.[32] She used a total of forty to forty-five pounds of flour, and for each five pounds of flour she put in two dozen whole eggs, a bit of salt, and a tiny amount of water (she looked at me rather incredulously when I asked for the *exact* proportion of water and salt, and said: "you just know by feeling what is the right amount and just put that in!"). After kneading the dough, Mrs. Bíró made small, tennis ball–sized forms, put these into stainless steel bowls, and covered the bowls with aluminum foil. The dough would "rest," she told me, until about eight o'clock, until the other noodle-makers arrived. One man, usually Mr. Steve Savel, then stretched the balls of dough with a rolling pin until each ball was shaped into a thin, foot-and-a-half-long flat shape. At that point two or three other men, or if on a particular Wednesday there were not enough men then a couple of men and a woman, placed these elongated flats into an Italian-made, manual crank-type pasta machine with which they stretched the dough even thinner, into elongated sheets. Yet another man cut these sheets into small, half-inch to three-quarter-inch squares. Still another man put these little square dough pieces onto ceramic plates, covered them with another plate, and delivered the plates full of dough squares to the long, white paper–covered tables where the women did the actual twirling of the snail-shaped soup garnish.

Women during csiga noodle making in the Great Hall of the Hungarian Reformed Church in Allen Park, Michigan (photo courtesy of Robert M. Darvas).

The women picked up the flat squares one at the time and laid them on their *csiga-borda*, or serrated boards where they twirled the squares into snail shapes, then dried them and bagged them for sale. Some of these boards were made of wood, others of reed, a few even of stainless steel, made at the Ford Motor Company by the husbands or sons of the women. Many were brought from Hungary by these women,

or by their mothers, grandmothers, or other natal female kin. The pride
of some of my informants in these implements cannot be properly
described: for instance, Mariska Leleszi (nee Csordás) very creatively
made her own *csiga-borda* from her long dead grandmother's ancient
szövőszék reed (weaving loom).

This is a continuously profitable version of women's work; from the
preparation and sale of the egg noodles the Women's Guild gives thousands of dollars to their parish.

Hungarian American Publications

To my knowledge, for at least a quarter century there has not been a
regularly published Hungarian language newspaper in Michigan.
Rather, those who want to read Hungarian language papers to keep up
with news of Hungary, and—more important—with other Hungarian
immigrant communities and national events order through the mail
one of the weekly papers from New York, Toronto, Cleveland, or Los
Angeles. According to Csilla Bartha's study, the most popular newspa-
pers among older Hungarian Americans in Michigan are the *Katoli-
kusok Vasárnapja (Catholics's Sunday)* and *Szabadság (Freedom)* from
Cleveland, the *Amerikai Magyar Szó (American Hungarian Word)* from
New York, the *Magyarság* and *Uj Szó (New Word)* from Toronto, and the
William Penn from Pennsylvania.[33]

Of course there are small local publications of the Hungarian
churches, for example in the Baptist Church of Reverend Géza
Herjeczky in Lincoln Park, the Hungarian Reformed Church in Allen
Park, and the Holy Cross Hungarian Roman Catholic Church in Delray.
These are primarily aimed at members of their respective congrega-
tions, however. The monthly newsletter of the Hungarian-American
Cultural Center (HACC) of Taylor serves as one of the only general,
locally written, duplicated, and distributed sources of news. One can
read about the center; find notices of births, marriages, and deaths, as
well as who had surgery, who is presently in the hospital, whose relatives are visiting from the Old Country, and who is visiting family in the
Old Country; and keep up to date on the many upcoming events, fund-
raisers and such in the center and elsewhere in the Hungarian

Performance of the Dancers Hungaria at the annual picnic of the Hungarian-American Cultural Center in Taylor, Michigan (photo courtesy of Robert M. Darvas).

American community. The newsletter is published in both Hungarian and English, with the specific aim of reaching and attracting younger members of the community. In addition, the HACC publishes an annual booklet each summer that is filled with advertisements for merchants and services in the community.

The Dancers Hungaria: Linda Enyedi and Violet Misángyi

One of the most important and lasting informal Hungarian associations in Michigan is the Dancers Hungaria, under the leadership of Linda Enyedi and Violet Misángyi. Both women are second-generation Hungarian Americans, very active in all things Hungarian, particularly in the Hungarian Arts Club and the dances. Linda is diligently refreshing her Hungarian, along with a number of others of the second, third, and even fourth generations, at one of the language classes offered at the HACC. While growing up, both women went with their parents to various Hungarian community events and listened to and loved the folk music and the group-folk and individual dances. They each started dancing in their teen years. Soon they were organizing a group, the Dancers Hungaria, and teaching the young people to do the many different regional dances of the Carpathian Basin. The highlight of the experience, Linda maintains, was the opportunity they had to visit Hungary and dance for and with the professional dancers in the Hungarian National Dance Ensemble.

Hungarian American Contributions to American Society

I fully agree with Hauk-Abonyi and Anderson that, while there were a large number of Hungarian Americans who contributed to nearly every field of endeavor, it is the people whose names are not known to posterity who were and continue to be the major contributors.[34] Those who worked underground in dangerous mines, those who took jobs in factories and foundries and worked the land, those who often suffered humiliation, those who often lived in poverty, and those who provided the backbone for the industrial development of the state of Michigan.

Of course, both Hungarians and Hungarian Americans are proud of their many Nobel Prize winners, including Albert Szent-Györgyi, who received the prize in 1937 for biochemistry, more specifically for discovering vitamin C in Hungarian paprika; György Békéssy, who received it for medicine and physiology in 1961; and Jenő (Eugene) Wígner and Dénes Gábor, who received the Nobel Prize for physics in 1963 and 1971, respectively. Imre Kertész was the 2002 winner of the Nobel Prize in Literature. Among the many Hungarian American developers, discoverers, and scientists are John von Neumann, who as one of the most remarkable mathematicians of his age was instrumental in the development of a proto-computer; Paul Erdős, the legendary mathemetician; Leó Szilárd, who patented the idea of nuclear chain reaction; Edward Teller, the father of the hydrogen bomb; Tódor (Theodor) von Kármán, who was instrumental in bringing in the Jet Age; Péter Károly Goldmark, who developed the long-playing record and the first color television; Béla Schick, who developed the diphteria diagnostic test and the Schick safety razor; Jónás Salk, who developed the polio vaccine; and Tivadar Puskás, who worked with Thomas Edison and invented the first telephone central switchboard. Hungarian Americans in the world of music are numerous. Among them are Béla Bartók, Jenő (Eugene) Ormándy, György Széll, Fritz Reiner, Antal Doráti, István Kertész, Ernő Dohnányi, Miklós Rózsa, Jenő (Eugene) Fodor, János Starker, József Szigeti, and Andrè Watts (son of an African American father and a Hungarian American mother). In the film industry there are Béla (William) Fox of Twentieth Century Fox; Adolf Zukor, the head of Paramount Studios; Béla Lugosi and Péter Lorre of horror film fame; Mitzi Gaynor, Paul Neuman, and Tony Curtis; the famous or infamous Gábor sisters, Zsazsa, Magda, and Éva, and their mother, Jolie Gábor; as well as Harry Houdini, who was born Erik Weiss in Budapest, the son of a Hungarian Jewish rabbi. In the field of literature there are the Baroness Orczy, who wrote the *Scarlet Pimpernel;* Ferenc Molnár, whose play entitled in Hungarian *Lilliom* became the musical *Carousel;* Edna Ferber; László Faragó; and a number of others. Other Hungarian contributors include József Pulitzer, the well-known publisher who established the prize named after him; the philosophers and economists Károly and Mihály; Polányi; philanthroper and financier György Soros; Andy Grove of Intel; and János Kornai, an economist at Harvard who developed the theory of "economics of shortage."[35]

There were a number of great contributors who lived and worked in Michigan. I will mention only a few, who were or still are in Michigan and contributed to our lives and our understanding of the world in which we live. József (Joseph) Galamb (1881–1955) designed the Model T and the Model A Ford and the Fordson tractor, invented the ignition plug and the planetary gearbox, and was instrumental in the production of Liberty aircraft engines. One of the most talented technical forebears of the American automotive industry, József Galamb had a very eventful career.[36] Zoltán Szepesy was director of Cranbrook as well as an artistin-residence. Ferenc Varga's bust of Ferenc Liszt is in Ford Auditorium and his figure of Pulaski is on Washington Boulevard in Detroit.

Among the Hungarian Americans at the University of Michigan of special achievement and world fame was Leslie Kish, who died at the age of ninety in late 2000. He was Professor Emeritus of Sociology and Statistical Mathematics at the University of Michigan and a member of the small group of social scientists who, in 1947, founded at the university the Institute for Social Research (ISR), the world's largest academic survey and research organization. He was widely recognized as one of the world's leading experts on scientific population sampling. His 1965 book, *Survey Sampling*, is still used around the world.

The superiority of the sampling techniques that Kish developed was first established in the 1948 U.S. presidential election. A small national probability sample of less than one thousand U.S. households drawn by Kish and his Michigan colleagues showed Dewey and Truman running very close together, with Truman slightly in the lead, while commercial polls and the press predicted a Dewey landslide.[37]

Textbooks by the brilliant geographer György Kiss are still used.

Let me also mention András Nagy, also know as Andrew F. Nagy, professor of space science and professor of electrical engineering at the University of Michigan. His research interests are the studies of the upper atmosphere, ionosphere, and magnetosphere of the Earth and other solar system bodies. Dr. Nagy was born in Budapest, Hungary. He received his M.S. degree in electrical engineering from the University of Nebraska in 1959 and his Ph.D. from the University of Michigan in 1963. "As a graduate student I was heading towards an electrical engineering career," he recalls, "when I was caught in the post-Sputnik excitement, which changed everything. It introduced me to the excitement of exploration. Given my engineering background, I was involved in the early direct measurements of the upper atmosphere. I also got interested in the environments of other solar system bodies. As we obtained more and more exciting new information from these measurements, I got interested in data interpretation and modeling of the environments of various solar system bodies."[38]

Hungarian Americans in Michigan at the Start of the Third Millennium

What Happened to Delray?

A gray-haired, rosy-faced, ever cheerful and affable merchant who weathered seven armed robberies and countless acts of vandalism in his Delray store, until he finally gave up and closed it in the mid-1990s, said to me in the late fall of 2001, "Delray is dead!" Indeed, the current appearance of Delray provides a sharp contrast to the image of the idyllic, flower-filled, peaceful community described by old informants and early documents and shown in old photographs. Today it is an urban slum, similar to those found in many American urban areas, where boarded up, burned out, abandoned houses, interspersed with weed-covered and trash-filled lots, dominate the scene. In the 1970s representatives of the African American, Hungarian, Mexican, and Puerto Rican ethnic groups that at the time populated the area organized "New Delray Incorporated," a group whose goals were to save and renovate the neighborhood. Its efforts appear to have been in vain: in spite of some improvements—including a police mini-station, a neighborhood city hall, and a small medical and mental health clinic—Delray today is a sad and dangerous place. "They have forgotten about us," I was told repeatedly. When I asked who *they* were, the old Hungarians-Americans just shrugged their shoulders and repeated themselves. **49**

Personal accounts and interviews reveal a continuous and frustrating struggle with the encompassing urban blight. The people express an overwhelming feeling of being trapped, inescapably stuck in a social environment over which they no longer have any control. Thus they live in fear, constantly under siege in an environment where vandalism, arson, burglaries, muggings, shootings, and knifings are common occurrences. Living behind heavily draped windows, behind chained and bolted doors, their telephones are their lifelines, the main vehicles for keeping in touch with one another and with their offspring. They are afraid to go outdoors; they walk to church together whenever they can, but only during the day. One small group gave up Tuesday evening prayer meetings because it was just becoming too dangerous to go out at night. Another had to forgo attending the weekly noodle-making sessions in the local Holy Cross Hungarian Roman Catholic Church for the same reason, after the treasurer of that church was robbed and beaten one morning in the parking lot. The few who still own automobiles in Delray have to chain them to the trunks of large trees. This way only the movable parts—batteries, hubcaps, windshield wipers, and antennas—will disappear overnight. Out of the literally hundreds of ethnic Hungarian social, cultural, and economic establishments constructed following the First World War, only the Roman Catholic Church and John K. Solosy's Mortuary remain open. The Hungarian Social Club of Detroit closed in the mid-1990s, after the cook-manager died. The priests at Holy Cross, the people at Solosy Funeral Home, and the handful of old Hungarian Americans appear to be holding steadfast. For the past couple of decades, as far as Hungarian life in Michigan is concerned, Delray during the weekdays appears to be increasingly marginal, forgotten, displaced. Already in the late 1980s one priest told me that "crime in the neighborhood is the worst we have ever seen. . . . when the church was broken into we were afraid for our lives."

A Detroit police sergeant who retired in the late 1980s after working for thirty-five years in the Detroit Police Department (DPD) Fourth Precinct, which includes Delray, said that there were only fifteen elderly Hungarians still living in the neighborhood.[39] What he called "the invasion" of various other ethnic groups had changed the close-knit

Christmas Mass in the Holy Cross Hungarian Roman Catholic Church (photo courtesy of Mihály Garazsi).

community forever. The Hungarians, he said, did not take well to members of these groups and, along with the rapidly increasing crime rate and growing drug problems, turf wars and gangs developed. The sergeant said that "the occurrence of Gypsy Fraud" was highest in the Delray area, as compared to other Detroit precincts, with home invasion and burglary following as the second most common crime.[40]

Another officer of the Fourth Precinct of the DPD said that "crime in this area is made up of purse snatching, muggings, crack houses, and more than its share of grand theft auto. Statistics over the years, and the monthly reports [of the DPD] have shown a dramatic increase of weapons possession, burglary, armed robberies, and larceny offenses and also homicide, rape, robbery, aggravated assault, and arson. But we have seen the biggest increase in drug-related crimes, including crack houses, robbery, and murder." The sergeant added that "many of the elderly people in neighborhood have been mugged by a drug buyer leaving a crack house and as they are walking down the street decide that they need some more money and hit and rob the elderly person."

One old couple, residents of Delray for more than six decades, simply refuses to leave. Mrs. Barabás told me that they tried it once for seven months, when she was unable to take care of her seriously ill husband and their daughter insisted that they move into her suburban house. Mrs. Barabás said that the daughter was just wonderful to them, yet they never felt at home there and simply felt homesick for the entire period they were away from Delray. When they moved back, "we knew immediately that we were where we belonged: at home."

Where are the other offspring of the people who feel "left behind"? Where are the newcomers? Where are the other tens of thousands we still find listed in the census as Hungarian American in and around the metropolitan area? They live in various suburbs of Detroit, though many go to church on Sundays and on special holidays, and for occasional visits to relatives in Delray on the weekends.

Yet, in spite of the danger and decay that I find difficult to describe without sounding melodramatic, Delray in some sense remains the symbolic center of the Hungarian American community for many people in southeastern Michigan. Although there is the Hungarian-American Cultural Center in Taylor, Michigan, and the Hungarian Reformed Church in Allen Park, just like all immigrant churches, has a "great room" available for all kinds of social gatherings, Hungarian Americans from a large region, including Detroit and suburbs, Windsor (Ontario), Flint, and many other areas in Michigan and northern Ohio, still gather in Delray for one of the most meaningful national holidays, the commemoration of the 1848 Revolution, in the middle of March. They also meet there for the annual Saint Stephen's Day celebration on the third weekend in August. On some Sundays hundreds, on other Sundays several dozens, of foreign-born as well as second- and third-generation Hungarian Americans drive in from the suburbs. They visit, and go to the services of Holy Cross Hungarian Roman Catholic Church, as others once attended the now defunct combined Hungarian Calvinist and Lutheran Church, the Byzantine Rite Catholic Church, and a number of other churches that are no longer there.

Amidst the depressing urban decay and apparent hopelessness and helplessness, there is still a sparkle of vibrant spirit among the Hungarian American inhabitants of Delray. This spirit emerges most explicitly in the stories about the occasional episodes when one of them has outsmarted a would-be robber, or thwarted an attempted break-in with what they call "just plain Hungarian cunning." These sto-ries are told and often repeated, much like traditional folk-tales, focus-ing on ingenuity, cleverness, and the triumph of good over evil. The protagonist's positive traits are always attributed to his or her specific ethnic identity, to being not only a Hungarian, but a Delray Hungarian. Other meaningful vestiges of this particular identity are frequently expressed in direct relationship to Delray, as if that neighborhood were the *végvár*, the last bastion, the fortress, the last outpost of what they call "real Hungarianness." As seventy-four-year-old Jolán Kéri told me, "Yes, the rich ones, who moved away from here, look down on us because we still live in Delray. But here we stayed real Hungarians, whereas they left their Hungarianness back here when they moved. If they want to feel good, they come back for a visit . . . they come and visit whenever they can, or call on the phone just to talk about the old days. They are lonely for us in those fancy suburbs. There they don't even know their neighbors."

Many conversations with former Delray residents show that, even if Mrs. Kéri exaggarates a bit, there is validity in her statement. For instance, the older people who moved away from the community refer to their present houses or apartments as *lakás*, meaning dwelling, liv-ing quarters, or residence, which has an emotionally neutral connota-tion, whereas they call their former Delray residences *otthon*, meaning home, which is an emotionally loaded term connoting warmth, belong-ing, hearth. There is ambivalence in their feelings about Delray. Their expressions of compassion, concern, and pity for kin, friends, and for-mer neighbors who "are left behind there" alternate with self-pity for no longer being a part of that community, and remorse that the commu-nity is no longer in existence. Then there is also among them a sense of self-satisfaction for selling their homes in time, "escaping" while it was still financially feasible. Former Delray residents still care about and know practically everything that occurs in that neighborhood. As so many have insisted, they do keep in touch, and they feel a certain painful longing, a nostalgia for Delray.

Thus, through the decades Hungarians in Delray created a self-consciously closed community around various ethnic churches and ethnic associations, but one that still maintained adaptive relationships with the larger world. The immigrants used multiple strategies to protect themselves from that world, and to survive in it. Even after the people began to move away from Delray to nearby suburbs—slowly at first in the years after the Second World War, and then rapidly after the urban riots of the 1960s—Delray in some sense remained the very center of Hungarian social, political, and economic activities. People regularly commuted from the suburbs to shop, visit, worship, and attend the many social and cultural functions. I have spoken with immigrants who were born and raised in Hungary after the communist takeover, knew very little of their Hungarian culture, and learned in Delray during the late 1950s and the 1960s, after emigrating from Hungary, elements like cooking, embroidery, and dancing that they consider to be part of a genuine Hungarian tradition.

While an estimated twelve thousand Hungarian-born individuals and their offspring still lived in Delray area during the early 1960s, the community was devastated by the riots in Detroit in the late 1960s.[41] The riots were followed by plummeting property values, by a major demographic and ethnic shift in the population, and, concomitantly, by the Hungarians' massive flight to nearby suburbs. By the 1980s, of the estimated twenty-seven thousand Hungarian Americans who lived in the Detroit metropolitan area, less than one hundred still resided in Delray. At the turn of the third millennium there were only about twenty-five. These were the people who did not "escape" to the suburbs fifteen, twenty, or twenty-five years ago, because they could not or would not leave their community. They were mainly elderly widows who lived on social security pensions.

Hungarian American Life outside Delray

Among other currently viable social institutions in Michigan, most prominent are the Hungarian-American Cultural Center (HACC) in Taylor; the Hungarian Reformed Church in Allen Park, particularly the Hungarian Heritage Preservation Circle; the branch of the Hungarian Reformed Federation in Lincoln Park; the Hungarian Baptist Church in Lincoln Park; the Szabolcs-Szatmár County Association of Allen Park; and the William Penn Association in Lincoln Park.

Just across the Detroit River is Windsor, and, as Zoltán Veres rightly asserts, "Insofar as Hungarians are concerned, Windsor-Detroit has been the Buda-Pest aspect of their lives.[42] As far back as the 1930s, skilled tradesmen who had emigrated to Canada opted to move [or regularly commute] to Detroit for better paying jobs, at tool and die [companies], Ford Motor Company, and so on.[43] . . . [In the social and cultural life of Hungarians in the two border cities,] residents had choices to make throughout the year."

When Mr. Veres talks about the current relationship between Hungarian immigrants in southeastern Michigan (he refers to them as "Detroiters") and those in the Windsor and Leamington regions of Ontario, he observes that "It is probably safe to say that more Detroiters frequent Windsor . . . than Windsorites going "the other way." Windsorites cite safety matters and the considerable difference in currency values. And of course since the middle of the 1990s, Detroiters are lured to Windsor because of the Casino and benefits of currency values. While Detroiters are here, they stock up on favorite food staples (salami, *kolbász* [Hungarian sausage], preserves, etc.). . . . In that respect the traffic of the 1930s from Windsor to Detroit . . . has been reversed."

The Hungarian-American Cultural Center and the Hungarian Reformed Church

A very wide variety of immigrants from various waves, and their offspring—second-, third-, and fourth-generation Hungarian Americans, Americans, and others—and people of all ages, from all walks of life, and from a wide geographical area of the Midwest regularly gather at the HACC. Several times each year formal and informal dances are held there, along with picnics, Gypsy festivals pig roasts, and traditional grape harvest celebrations. At these events, in addition to the Hungarian food, dance programs by the Csipke-Dance Group and Dancers Hungaria, and both live and recorded music, networks of friends, families, and compatriots not only from throughout the state of Michigan but also frequently from Ohio, Indiana, Ontario, and elsewhere are reactivated. Furthermore, each year at the HACC one can hear Hungarian poetry readings, lectures, and live music. On occasion, plays, cabarets, and films are shown, again amid the rich display of Hungarian material culture. The Hungarian choir of the area regularly meets there, as do the Csipke-Dance Group and Dancers Hungaria for weekly practices. Hungarian language classes are also regularly held at the center. As in the past, the importance of women today in maintaining the community cannot be overstated. As a newcomer said, "not only do the women participate, but they work harder, and make all the decisions. The men don't like to hear this, but it is true. Whenever there are fund-raisers, men delegate most chores to us women."

Another vital center of current Hungarian American life in Michigan is the Hungarian Reformed Church in Allen Park. Immigrants from the different waves and their offspring become particularly active in the various associations after they retire. They participate in voluntary associations, some without paying too much attention to their Hungarian ancestry or the lack thereof, as well as others who, as I have already discussed, explicitly identify themselves as "Wednesday Hungarians."[44] Cooking, baking, bake sales, fund-raising dinners, and similar food-related activities were and remain crucially important in the Hungarian American communities of Michigan, illustrating the ongoing significance of foodways and the meanings attached to them in the maintenance of symbolic ethnic identity.[45] Many are also active in the Church Council, the Dorcas Guild, and the Szabolcs-Szatmár County Association.[46] Some belong to the Women's Fellowship Organization, and to the Hungarian Heritage Preservation Circle, whose founders are the newcomers from Transylvania.

Until 1990 the Hungarian Club of Detroit, on Jefferson, in the center of Delray, continued to sponsor an annual three-day festival held at Wyandotte's Yack Arena where many thousands got together to eat, drink, dance, and listen to the music. In 1991 the Holy Cross Hungarian Roman Catholic parish took over the organization of that important festival, and this parish continues to hold it.

Members of the Hungarian Arts Club of Detroit are still very active. The club was formed in 1958, and, as they describe it, they are "dedicated to preserving Hungarian heritage and supporting the arts." In addition, they sponsor concerts for touring groups from Hungary and elsewhere from the Carpathian Basin, and annually award scholarships

Members of the Hungarian-American Cultural Center on a winter afternoon in Taylor, Michigan (photo courtesy of Robert M. Darvas).

to students of Hungarian descent studying the fine arts. They also host the annual White Rose Ball.

The Hungarian Film Club was started in the fall of 2002 by a couple of brave and enthusiastic Ann Arborites. The screenings of recent Hungarian films with English subtitles are followed by discussions and casual visiting. The young president of the Film Club received an award of recognition from Washtenaw Community College for his diligent work and success in reaching out not only to the Hungarian ethnic community but to film-lovers of all ethnicity in an area that is much larger than Washtenaw County; families drive from elsewhere in Michigan, Ohio, and Windsor to enjoy the films and discussions that are open to the public.

Hungarian American Burial Methods in Michigan

According to cross-cultural studies on death and funeral customs, these are the most lasting types of customs, the most resistant to change. This does not seem to be the case among Hungarian Americans in

Michigan.[47] Most funeral customs are unequal amalgamates of American and rural Hungarian customs, and there is much more of the former than the latter, in spite of the fact that, not counting churches, the oldest continuous (and still existing, even if not flourishing) Hungarian ethnic enterprises in Lincoln Park and Delray are the Solosy, and in Brownstown the Molnar funeral homes. Indeed, many elements of funeral and cemetery culture, as well as attitudes toward and about death, particularly the abundant use of euphemism, are similar to the American ways. One of the funeral directors commented that even though religious groups stay together and bury their dead within the rites of their respective churches, Hungarian American funerals are increasingly similar to American funerals. For example, one woman who emigrated from Hungary in the early 1970s recalled that "here they only say good things about the dead [not the truth], and the so-called mourners start chatting and giggling right after the ceremony is over, even around the open coffin."

Regarding funeral customs among Hungarian Americans, one of the priests said that

> I left Hungary in 1939 . . . [and] came to this country in 1946 . . . but I still [clearly] remember my uncle's funeral in the village. Oh, I was about seven or eight at the time. That was my first experience with death in the family or attending a funeral. . . . My grandpa took me and I was very impressed by the . . . singing and all. . . . It was a beautiful, natural expression, unadorned and unpainted, and open. Just the soul going to the Lord Jesus. . . . In 1947 [here in Delray] I went to see an old person, a very sick and miserable one and gave her the Sacrament of Anointing and then prayed near her. She died and a week later there was the funeral. I was really surprised to see that she was so very beautiful, unusually so, in the coffin. Everything was so beautiful, so serene, so attractive about her and around her too. There was one of the Brothers [I think here he meant fellow priest] with me and I said to him, "Gee, maybe that is from the inner attitude of the woman. She must have been a holy person, she was a good [woman] and now this [shows through], in death." [The Brother said to me,] "Oh, you are so naïve . . . don't be so naïve! She has been prepared by the funeral direc-

tor. . . ." Here they embalm, they put on paint. . . . There was nothing like that in Hungary . . . here in America the funeral is a business and [the business is to] cover up the reality of death.[48]

Contrary to prevailing customs in Hungary, here there are very few expensive, ornate, and large gravestones. When a student of mine asked a Hungarian American the reason for this difference, he answered, "Here, we always cry that we are poor. Over there we are really poor, but we show our riches."

In the early 2000s, while attending a friend's funeral in an Ann Arbor cemetery, I noticed a large, red, white, and green decorated box of sweet paprika from the southern Hungarian city of Szeged on top of a flat, granite gravestone with a Hungarian name on it.[49] Shortly thereafter in a Milan, Michigan, cemetery I saw what I must call the most remarkable manifestation of dual identity, American and Hungarian, expressed even from beyond the grave. Around the grave there were red, white, and green flowers. On the very top of the almost monument-size, dark granite stone was a statue of the deceased's favorite cat, Butzi. On one side of the stone there were two engraved, intercrossed flags, an American and a Hungarian; below this were the name, birth date and death date of the deceased; and underneath this were the name and birthday of his widow. On the opposite side of the stone, using a para-phrased English translation from a poem of Sándor Petőfi, a well-known nineteenth-century Hungarian poet and revolutionary, was the explicit proclamation of the dual identity of the man in the grave.

Hungarian American into the Future: Prospects for Michigan's Hungarians

The last couple of waves of immigrants neither incorporated into, unified, nor revitalized the aging and diminishing community of Hungarian Americans in Michigan. Nevertheless, they formed a vital organization through which they perpetuate selected cultural elements. Many of the now older, second- and third-generation immigrants who were born and raised in Delray maintain their symbolic ethnic identity. They continue to display selected customs, foodways, terms of communication, and patterns of social relationships learned from either their immigrant parents or other kin. These, however, are not only carefully selected elements of a specifically Delray-Hungarian culture and social form, but they are also situationally practiced and displayed. In other words, these ways and patterns are not incorporated into everyday lives, as they were among the immigrants and those children of immigrants who lived their lives within the ethnic community. Rather, these descendents of immigrants express their ethnicity, their Hungarianness on weekends or on holidays in such a manner that most often they fit what Herbert Ganz has called the second, third, and subsequent generations' symbolic ethnicity. For example, this situational and symbolic ethnicity is clearly articulated by the women who call themselves "Wednesday Hungarians." Nevertheless, this symbolic and situational expression of ethnic identity is meaningful and therefore highly significant in the lives of these second- and third-generation Hungarian Americans. As in the cases of the two sisters described in appendix 2, selected elements of Delray socialization and childhood have been well integrated into the "American ways" of life of these second- and third-generation immigrants, and they continue to function later in life as important sources of activities and relationships. I found a similar pattern in other Michigan communities that once had large and thriving Hungarian communities—for example, in Flint and Burton. Foods, holidays, festivals, church socials, and similar events help to maintain and perpetuate a culture that is neither Hungarian nor American but a specific Michigan-style Hungarian American. Like Zoltán Veres, I would like to be positive yet remain realistic about the future of Hungarian American ethnic life in our region. He is cautious but still predicts that

> the tradition and the beat goes on. And the Windsor-Detroit [Hungarian] connection will survive for as long as Hungarian churches and cultural activities exist. That, as it is and will be with most ethnic groups, will be the challenge of the new millennium.

Anna Kovács's Story (excerpts)

The following passage is from one of the several hundred life histories I gathered during my more than two decades of ethnographic fieldwork among Hungarian Americans in Michigan.[50] Mrs. Kovács is but one of many hundreds of thousands of Hungarian Americans who were forced by economic or political necessity to flee her homeland and try to piece together a new life in Michigan during the past century. Her story is not at all intended to be exemplary of the "typical life experience" of Hungarians who came to Michigan, but many of its themes do reflect common problems of this and other groups in the early years of adjustment. I found this woman an excellent informant, articulate, lucid, direct, honest. The multiple leitmotifs of her story—hard work; marital difficulties; alcoholism; the exploitation of women in the factories, in the shops, and in the home; the crucial importance of relationships; the sense of loss at being cut adrift from her natal family, language, and culture; and networking with fellow villagers as one of many strategies of adaptation—were not uncommon. A number of other life stories I collected, as well as Erdmann Beynon's studies, show similar patterns. Therefore, while indeed there is no such thing as the typical immigrant experience, I found Anna Kovács's story particularly significant because it spans more than seven decades, from early 1912 **61** until the middle of the 1980s, when, shortly before she died, I recorded her story.

> I never forget how very cold it was that early February night in 1912 when we got to Delray. It was nearly midnight, yet it was shiny, so beautiful with all the stores lit up on Jefferson, and those *streetkárész* [streetcars] going back and forth. . . . First, my husband and I stayed with fellow villagers from Aldebrő, who owned two houses already. Another young couple from my village, six children of my aunt, and who knows how many boarders lived in the same house by the time we moved in. Then, when my best friend from my village arrived in Delray, we moved in with them, to another boardinghouse. You see, my father was here already, once again, by the time we got to Detroit in 1912. He worked as a skilled worker in Solvay Company and lived in a boardinghouse on Medina Street. I was not on good terms with him. He drank too much, always just drank and caroused, only once he sent some money to my mother, who remained in the village. He never went to work on Mondays, just drank and spent his time with women. Incidentally, that way he survived the biggest industrial accident in which lots of workers, Hungarians among them, died in Solvay plant. He was so proud! He kept repeating to everybody how he stayed alive by sitting and drinking at the corner saloon when he was supposed to be working. My first husband was just like him too. I had to work, could never really count on him. Two days after we got here I had a job already. I had to do everything: first I worked in the foundry here, but conditions were very bad, so I left and went to work in a laundry over on Jefferson. I started with three dollars a week, then, when I did fancy work, you know lacy little dresses and cloths, I earned twelve dollars. . . . My son, Ferenc József, was born a year after we got here. I stayed home with him for a little while, but we needed the money. And even though I was sewing for people after he was born and did earn a little that way, we needed more. When the First War broke out I became a core-maker in a local factory. I made good money, fifteen dollars a week. . . . After the War, I lost that job and went back sewing for a Hungarian Jewish shop in Delray. But they did not pay enough, so I went to work for a furrier . . . then between 1932 and 1943 I was sewing

for Hudson's [Department Store]. We even opened a grocery and butcher shop right here on West End Street, but my first husband liked to run over to the corner saloon, rather than work in the store, so we could not make a go of that either. Then my son married in 1936, a girl from Budapest, who was living right here in Delray with her family. So, I stayed here alone with the lazy drunkard, who did not care if we get thrown out to the street. Finally I divorced him in 1940, but my son, neighbors, and relatives would never let me live that down. To this day they are mad at me because of the divorce and of course because I married István Nagy soon thereafter. . . . István was set OK, he had two rooming houses and we always had good roomers, so we did not have financial worries. But that one . . . liked to socialize too much with his fellow Szatmár County Hungarians here. But at least he respected me, so that marriage was a proper one. But my first husband, Lord he was cruel, he hit me, he lied to me, and even when he worked he spent his money in the saloon and then laughed with his buddies about how he cheats his wife out of everything. I never had any real joy in my life, but the most unhappy times I had was during my first marriage here, when we could not get ahead, because of his constant drinking. . . . I was nearly fifty when I married my second husband, you see, and until then I alone had to provide for the family. . . . He [the second husband] did not have any children, he was frugal and knew how to treat money really well . . . we should have sold this house [in Delray] long ago, but even after he got a stroke, and . . . died in 1965, I did not sell. I am very attached to this lot here, the yard and gardening mean so much to me. . . . I missed it when I went home, I mean [back] to Hungary. . . . The first time I went back was in '28. My mother and all my siblings were still alive then. I remember, how people changed by '28. I wanted to talk and visit, but there was always too much work to do and there were no servants by then. When we visited Budapest I was very disappointed, those city folks are so cold, so heartless. I cannot even tell you why I went back in '68 and '73. Only one of my sisters was alive by then, she was sickly, but we visited Eger and that was nice. But everything changed there, it was really strange for me. . . . All my life I always worked, never looked outside for things to do. I like to do my gardening the most, and listen to the news on radio and television. . . . While

I never learned to talk in English really well (I got along with Hungarian just fine around here), I do read it and understand it. So now I just rather read, or listen to the radio by myself. . . . My real friends are almost all gone. There used to be thirteen of us here, all from my home village. We got together for dinner regularly, twice a month and that I liked. Now it is hard to get together anymore: those who are still alive from among us are either in nursing homes or in apartments in the suburbs. And so many of my friends and fellow villagers died already. Well, so we are all slowly disappearing.

Socialization Processes of Immigrants' Children

The first of the following excerpts is from the life story of Mariska Leleszi.[51] She was one of those relatively rare parents here who already in the 1940s and 1950s encouraged and supported her children to become professionals. However, while she is very proud of her children's professional and financial success, at the same time she also bemoans their lack of interest in "anything Hungarian," and she consciously perceives this as a discontinuity of something meaningful. She interprets "the children being *too* Americanized" as her failure as a generative parent. For example, while showing me an old, smooth rolling pin in her spotless and cheery kitchen she said,

> this belonged to my mother-in-law. Bless her soul, she has been dead now for quite a few years. She told me that the first time she came to America it was the only thing she could not leave behind. Then she went back and forth, five different times, and took her rolling pin with her each time. I married her one and only son, and, of course, I inherited her rolling pin. I am still using it. . . . But I know that while the rolling pin will stay with one of my (three) children after I die, they will never use it. They don't make noodles like we do. Us, our generation,

my generation is the last one . . . the children are too Americanized.
My granddaughter, who is eighteen now, is interested in cooking,
especially in preparing fast dishes. They say they don't have time, they
don't do stuff like noodle making. Perhaps this is our fault. They are
professional people. My husband and I stressed education to my children. For them to study was the most important thing, we said. When
they came home from school, supper was either all ready or partially
prepared. . . . They did not have to learn our ways, how to make noodles or bread. . . . You see, my dear, for me it was different. When I
came to America [at the age of thirteen] my mother had boarders. I
had to learn how to make noodles and bread. . . . I had to drop out of
school [after the sixth grade] and stay home to help.

The second excerpt contains fragments of conversations I had at
one of the many noodle-making sessions. During these meetings
women often talked about their childhood in Delray and emphasized
that these sessions meant a meaningful sense of continuity in their
lives. I talked with two widowed sisters, born in 1911 and 1912 in Filbert,
West Virginia, of parents who emigrated in 1909 from Szabolcs County,
and raised in Delray after the family moved to Michigan. Viktória, the
older of the two sisters, recalled that

[W]hen mother died . . . she impressed it upon us on her deathbed,
"don't leave your church, do go regularly, do your work there properly."
The church was mother's life before she got so sick, you see. Besides,
we both feel very comfortable here on Wednesdays among the
Hungarian ladies. . . . We like the social aspect of the church. . . . Even
though we often do not make it for the Sunday [formal church] services, we make sure to be here every Wednesday for the noodle-making
[sessions], and we always help prepare for all the big church suppers
and [other] fund-raising events too.

Often women related csiga noodle making with their own upbring-
ing. They asserted that they were continuing something they had
learned as very young children either in the Hungarian village or in the
United States from their Hungarian-born mothers, grandmothers, or

Hungarian immigrants arriving in New York on the SS Europa from Bremen on 21 March 1930. Mariska (Mary) Csordás (subsequently Mrs. Mary Leleszi) is crouching while holding the "Europa" sign. Her sister, Juliska Csordás, is standing on the left side of the photograph, in a white blouse. The ship made record time, crossing from Bremen to New York across the Atlantic Ocean in four days (photograph courtesy of Mariska Leleszi, née Csordás).

other female natal kin. Recalling her childhood in Delray, Ilona, the younger sister of the woman cited in the preceding text, said that

> Grandmother had a nice philosophy about raising us. She said that we
> must properly learn everything as children, so we could become
> decent and diligent adults. She taught us how to knead dough, and
> how to make *csiga* even before we could reach the top of the kitchen
> table without the help of standing on a bench.

Complaints that children of today are not brought up as well as the preceding generations are universal and timeless. In any ethnic community these complaints are more emphasized, not only because of differences between generations, but also because the way children were socialized in the villages of the Old Country are rarely if ever appropriate in the urban setting of what Kósa called the "land of choice." Indeed, as many men and women told me, the transmission of "proper Hungarian ways" from one generation to the next was a major problem, a never-ending and complex struggle. Most children of immigrants live between two very different worlds, what Iván Sanders calls between languages and between cultures, and they try to negotiate between these worlds. This is illustrated by the following story of socialization in Delray, told from the perspectives of a second-generation immigrant. This is the account of sixty-year-old Aranka Tóth, who never married, and at the time of our conversations still lived with her ninety-year-old mother in the small Delray house where she was born. Aranka said that

the first thing I learned was to pay my respect to old people. My brothers and I had to greet all old folks first, and we had to call them all *néni* or *bácsi*, [aunt or uncle], whether or not they were related to our family. Mother said, "Don't you ever make fun of anybody who is older than you are, or I'll skin you alive!" My brother made fun of this old woman, who lived down from us here on South Street, she was the ugliest one in all of Delray. Boy, did he get a hiding from our Mom! . . . Another thing that was impressed upon us early in life was to be home at six o'clock, when the church bells chimed. The whole family had to be in the house, no matter what, and we all prayed together, then sat down to dinner together. . . . All of us children had small jobs by the time we were ten years old. My older brother worked in the Molnár Funeral Parlor, he was doing odd jobs, washed cars, swept the sidewalk, and stuff like that by the time he was eleven. When he outgrew that job, we inherited it with my other brother. . . . Of course, like all the other kids from Delray, we attended the American elementary, junior, and high schools, where we were called the Hunkies, and the kids often laughed at my name too, and they made fun of how my mother dressed me. Like the other Hungarian kids, we went to Hungarian-language school, too, at our church, Holy Cross Hungarian Roman Catholic Church. . . . I did not speak English when I started school, but that came quickly. . . . I never learned to read or write in Hungarian although I went to the Hungarian-language school for six years here at Holy Cross. There were many activities for kids and teenagers at our church as I was growing up. My brothers and I were in every play, every choir in the church. . . . I still am very active, now I am the president of the Ladies' Rosary Group and I attend every funeral from our parish with the rosary, of course. . . . I had to speak Hungarian with my grandparents, who lived with us, and now that my mother is old and often is confused we speak only Hungarian between us anymore. . . . Still, by the time I was a teenager it was somehow easier for me to speak English than Hungarian.

Six Hungarian Recipes

Gulyás Soup (goulash) and Csipetke (small pinched noodles)

3 Tbsp. oil

3 medium onions, peeled and chopped

3 lbs. lean beef, cubed into ¾-inch pieces

3 Tbsp. sweet Hungarian Paprika

1 tsp. hot Hungarian Paprika

2 garlic cloves, peeled and minced

1 tsp. caraway seeds, or 2 tsp. powdered caraway

salt to taste

1½ lbs. potatoes, peeled, washed, and cubed into ¾-inch pieces

1 tomato (optional)

1 white sweet Hungarian pepper (optional)

Use a heavy, large (at least six-quart capacity) kettle for this dish. Sauté onions in oil until light golden.

Add the cubed beef, stir well, and cook on low heat for 15 minutes. Carefully stirring, so paprika will not burn, add both kinds of paprika, the garlic, caraway, salt, and 3 quarts of warm water. Cover and cook over low heat for 1 hour (cooking time depends on the cut of the meat).

Add the cubed potatoes (and, if you like, also add the optional ingredients, the cubed tomato and sliced pepper) and cook for another 35 minutes. Then taste, and add salt if needed.

Finally, cook a handful of Csipetke (recipe follows) into the Gulyás. Meal will be ready to eat when the Csipetke rise to the surface of the Gulyás, after about 7–10 minutes cooking. *Serves 8–10 people.*

Csipetke (small pinched noodles)

⅓ cup all-purpose flour
2 egg yolks
pinch of salt

Make a very hard dough out of the ingredients. Add more flour if needed. Let dough rest for a few minutes, then pinch and twist little pieces between the thumb and forefinger and cook these Csipetke in the slowly cooking Gulyás before serving. *Makes 1½ cups.*

Notes: Genuine Hungarian Gulyás should have the consistency of a rich, thick soup and be served in a soup bowl and eaten with a soup spoon. It is not a stew, like most American dishes that are called "gulash."

Instead of the beef, bite-sized pieces of mutton, pork, or veal can be substituted.

The dish is also tasty when it is made without any meat. The same recipe without meat is called Hamis Gulyás, or Mock Gulyás. When 16 ounces of presoaked pinto beans or white beans are substituted for both the meat and potatoes, the dish is called Bab Gulyás, or Bean Gulyás.

George Lang, in his excellent *The Cuisine of Hungary*—a work that I consider both much more than a mere cookbook, because it is an excellent and not ethnocentric history of the cuisine of the Carpathian Basin, and a much-less-than-good cookbook, because it lacks simple Hungarian recipes—calls Gulyás, pörkölt, paprikás, and tokány "the four pillars of Hungarian cooking."

Lang's warning must be heeded when attempting to cook any Hungarian dish: Spanish paprika should never be substituted for Hungarian! The former is merely a coloring agent, while the latter gives the flavor, substance, and aroma for which Hungarian cooking is well-known.

Most Hungarians would consider a bowl of Gulyás served with a slice of crusty dark or light rye bread and followed by a noodle dessert dish (see Rakott Metélt) a satisfying, full evening or noon meal.

Székely Gulyás, or Székely Káposzta (Székely Gulyás, or Székely Cabbage)

2 Tbsp. oil
2 medium onions, peeled and finely chopped
3 lbs. of lean pork, cubed into ½-inch pieces
3 Tbsp. sweet Hungarian Paprika
3 lbs. sauerkraut
2 garlic cloves, peeled and minced
1 tsp. caraway seed, or 2 tsp. powdered caraway
salt to taste
2 cups sour cream mixed with 2 Tbsp. milk

Sauté onion in oil until light. Add cubed pork, cover, and cook for 10 minutes. Add paprika, caraway seed, and 2 tablespoons water. Cook over low heat until almost done.

With cold water slightly rinse sauerkraut (if it is too salty, soak in cold water for a few minutes) then squeeze well. Add to the meat and cook for 30 minutes. Add salt to taste. Mix 2 tablespoons milk with 1½ cups of sour cream, add to dish, and cook until it comes to a slight boil.

Just before serving, top each individual portion of Székely Káposzta with a dollop of sour cream. Serve this dish with good crusty dark or light rye bread. *Serves 8.*

Csirke Paprikás (Hungarian Chicken Paprikás)

2 medium onions, very finely chopped
3 Tbsp. cooking oil, or chicken or pork fat (i.e., lard)
4 Tbsp. genuine sweet paprika
2 tsp. salt
5–6 lbs. chicken legs or thighs
1 cup water
1 pint sour cream (if too thick, mix with a couple of Tbsp. milk)

Sauté onions in shortening until light golden brown. Add paprika, salt, and chicken pieces that have been washed and patted semidry, and cook for 15–20 minutes. Add water, cover, and let simmer slowly until it is tender, about 30 more minutes (length of time depends on the types of chicken pieces; if you use chicken breasts they cook longer than thighs and legs). Remove chicken pieces, add the sour cream to the sauce, and mix until smooth. Boil very briefly and put chicken pieces back into the sauce.

Serve with dumplings, rice, or pasta, and Hungarian cucumber salad. *Serves 8–10.*

Kolozsvári Rakott Káposztás Kacsacomb (Layered Sauerkraut and Duck Thighs ala Kolozsvár [Cluj-Napoca]) and Tarhonya

> 10 pieces of duck legs and thighs, or breasts (best are Amish duck legs)
>
> 3 garlic cloves, peeled
>
> 10 oz. smoked bacon, thinly sliced (optional)
>
> 3 quarts of good quality sauerkraut
>
> 16 oz. sour cream mixed with ½ cup milk
>
> salt
>
> ground black pepper

After rinsing and drying duck pieces, salt and pepper the pieces and put them single-layered into a baking pan. Add a ½ cup of water and the whole garlic cloves and bake in a 375° oven for about 50 minutes.

Rub a piece of bacon in the inside of a 2-inch-deep casserole dish, and layer half of the thinly sliced bacon, half of the sauerkraut, all the duck pieces, and the other half of the sauerkraut into the dish. Finally, pour on and evenly distribute the sour cream-milk mixture, and then cover with the other half of the bacon. Bake this for 1 hour at 350°. Brown the top carefully in the last 10 minutes, and crisp the top layer of bacon.

Serve this dish with a good crusty dark or light rye bread and with tarhonya, jasmine rice, or any small pasta. *Serves 8–10.*

Tarhonya

16 oz. of tarhonya (or jasmine rice or other small pasta)
2 Tbsp. oil
2 Tbsp. margarine
30 oz. *hot* chicken stock (or water; 20 oz. if using jasmine rice)
salt to taste

To prepare tarhonya, brown pasta or rice in oil and margarine, carefully stirring all the time. When it becomes a nice golden brown, add 30 ounces of *hot* chicken stock or water. Add salt to taste, and cook on low heat, tightly covered, until tender. It takes 30–35 minutes for the tarhonya to cook, or about 25 minutes for the jasmine rice to cook. Fluff with fork and taste before serving.

Notes: Kolozsvári Rakott Káposztás Kacsacomb—just like good wine and good women—improves with age. Similar to other cabbage and sauerkraut dishes, it is best when served on the second, third, or even the fourth day following preparation. And, much to my surprise, even freezing did not ruin the quality of this dish.

Tarhonya can be purchased at most European delicatessens, or can be substituted for by a small, round Italian egg pasta, or similar small pasta.

Rakott Metélt (Layered Noodle Dessert)

5 cups milk
pinch of salt
½ lb. unsalted butter
3-inch piece of vanilla bean
1 lb. wide, high-quality egg noodles (fresh pasta would be best)
4 large Granny Smith Apples, cored, peeled, and quartered
1 cup sugar
rind of one whole lemon
5 eggs, separated
1 cup white raisins
¼ cup bread crumbs

1 cup ground hazelnuts, almonds, or walnuts

3 Tbsp. lemon juice

Cook for 5 minutes over low heat the milk, salt, 2 tablespoons of the butter, and vanilla bean. Add the noodles and cook for 12–15 minutes, stirring continuously. All the liquid should be absorbed by the end of this process.

Cook in another pot the quartered apples in a spoonful of sugar and a cup of water for about 10 minutes. Apples should not be thoroughly cooked. Pat dry.

Reserve 4 tablespoons. of sugar to be combined with egg whites and lemon juice. Beat well remaining butter and sugar with the lemon rind and the five egg yolks. Gently mix in the raisins.

Butter a deep baking dish and sprinkle it with bread crumbs. Put in half of the cooked noodles and then the apples. Sprinkle the ground hazelnuts (or ground almonds) on top of the apples, cover with the remaining noodles, and bake at 350° for 30 minutes.

Beat the egg whites with 4 Tbs. sugar and the lemon juice. Pour this meringue on top of the noodles and bake for 12–15 minutes, until meringue is a light golden color. *Serves 8–10.*

Finom Vajas Kifli (Kati Horváth's fine butter crescent cookies)

1 lb. unsalted butter, at room temperature

4 Tbsp. Crisco shortening

juice of a large lemon

8 Tbsp. sour cream

13 egg yolks

5 cups of all-purpose flour

sweet chestnut, poppy seed, or walnut pastes, or thick and tart
apricot, plum, or other jam for filling

Combine all ingredients and knead until elastic-like dough is obtained. Form the dough into medium apple–sized balls, cover well with wax paper, and refrigerate overnight (or pack thoroughly and freeze until ready to bake).

Remove dough balls, one at the time, from the refrigerator, and using a cold rolling pin, stretch each ball into a circle that is about 10 to 12 inches in diameter. With a pizza cutter cut into eight wedges. Place about ⅓ teaspoons of filling onto each wedge and roll them up, starting at the wider end. Pinch the ends and bend cookies into crescent shape. Bake on ungreased cookie sheet at 350° for 12–15 minutes, until crescents are light golden brown. While still warm, roll each crescent in powdered sugar. *Makes about 120 crescent cookies.*

Notes: I would like to dedicate this recipe to the memory of Katalin Horváth, who prepared it more times than I could count for the various functions at the HACC in Taylor and elsewhere. This very dynamic, generous, and community-spirited Hungarian American woman gave me this version of this widely used recipe a couple of years before she died, unexpectedly and prematurely.

There is no denying that there is work with this recipe, but it is well worth the bother. I usually get over a hundred and twenty crescents out of these ingredients. The dough stores well in the freezer, as do the already baked crescents. For unexpected guests I have popped some of these crescents while frozen into the microwave oven for just 25–35 seconds, without loss of flavor or of the quality of this subtle, fine, buttery pastry.

Filling can be simplified by purchasing SOLO brand ground and sweetened poppyseed, apricot, or prune filling.

When rolling dough into circles, use either wax paper or a marble slab, so it will not stick.

Hungarian American Annual Calendar of Events

February: The Hungarian Arts Club of Detroit holds its Annual White Rose Ball on the first Saturday of February. This is a formal event, usually held in the Dearborn Inn, where debutantes of Hungarian descent are introduced and with their escorts they dance a traditional Hungarian dance, the *palotás*. Every year members of the Arts Club find a student of Hungarian ancestry who is in art studies and shows promise, and give the student a generous check.[52]

March: The anniversary of the Hungarian Revolution of 1848 and the War of Independence that followed is celebrated each year on the closest Sunday to the 15th of March in the Márton Áron Hall (formerly known as the Marble Hall) of the Holy Cross Roman Catholic Church in Delray. This celebration is sponsored and organized by members of the Federation of Hungarian Churches, Clubs, and Societies, an umbrella organization that—as its name implies—aims to embrace all the religious and secular institutions in the area.

May: The Spring Poetry and Literary Afternoon is held annually, and is organized by Mr. János Stubits, the president of the Freedom Fighters Association of Detroit, and Mrs. Emmi Stubits.

June: A two-day weekend summer picnic is held on the grounds of the HACC.

June: The Hungarian Festival is held at the Yack Arena in Wyandotte, organized and sponsored by the Holy Cross Roman Catholic Church.

June: (usually on two weekends) The Carrousel of Nations is sponsored by the Multicultural Council of Windsor, Ontario, and held in Windsor, where "Hungarian villages" are usually set up.

July: The so-called Gypsy Picnic is held on the grounds of the HACC.

August 20th, or the closest weekend to the 20th: Saint Stephen Day celebrations are held at the Holy Cross Roman Catholic Church in Delray, organized by the priests of that church and their committees.

September: The Fall Festival Pig Roast, a picnic-like fund-raising event, including a barbecue, musicians, and the Dancers Hungaria is held on the grounds of the HACC.

October, nearest Sunday to the 23rd: A commemoration of the October Revolution of 1956 that is organized by the Hungarian Freedom Fighters Association under the leadership of Mr. János Stubits and Mrs. Emmi Stubits and held at the HACC.

October: Grape Harvest Dances are held at the Hungarian Reformed Church in Allen Park, at the HACC, and at the Mindszenty Hall in Windsor, Ontario.

November: The Budapest Ball is held at the HACC and organized by Mr. and Mrs. János Stubits.

December, the first or second Saturday: The Borbála Dance is held at the HACC and organized by a DP voluntary association, the Federation of Hungarian Veteran (MHBK).

December 6th: Saint Nicholas Day gathering is held for children at the HACC and the various Hungarian American churches.

December 31: Szilvester dance, or New Year's Eve dance is held in the HACC.

First and third Sundays of each month: Between early September and late May, on the first and third Sundays of each month, Hungarian films with English subtitles are shown at the Washtenaw Community College, in auditorium LA 175. These screenings start at 6:00 P.M. and are followed by informal discussions. Both the founder and the president of the Film Club aim to preserve and perpetuate selected elements of Hungarian culture. For example, a Saint Nicholas Day celebration for children, a Christmas celebration, and a Hungarian Easter celebration have been organized. For more information, e-mail *arttour@prodigy.net.*

Actually, there are many more spontaneous events than I was able to list here. Hardly a week goes by when there is not either an impromptu fund-raising dinner; a private gathering, such a wake, a baby shower or a wedding-shower; or an actual celebration of a wedding, baptism, anniversary, or some other function. The private gatherings are often not so private, because they can include up to a couple hundred Hungarian Americans from the local community and far beyond. There are dinners at the HACC each Friday between 5 P.M. and 8 P.M. and the first Sunday of each month between noon and 7 P.M. These are open to the public.

Notes

I am most appreciative for Mrs. Helen Kulcsár for giving me Tibor Tóth's *Historical Album for the Dedication of the Hungarian Reformed Church* (Detroit: Pálos Press, 1941).

1. Excerpt from Attila József's poem entitled "Hazám" (My homeland), in *Complete Works of Attila József* (Budapest: Szépirodalmi Kiadó, 1980), 443.
2. In the section that follows I used data from Éva Huseby-Darvas, "Hungarians," in *The Encylclopedia of World Cultures*, ed. David Levinson (New Haven, Conn.: Yale University Press, 1992), 2:142–45; Éva Huseby-Darvas, "Hungarian Americans," in *American Immigrant Cultures: Builders of a Nation*, ed. David Levinson and Melvin Ember (London: Macmillan Reference Library, 1997), 1:401–10; Éva Huseby-Darvas, "Hungarian," in *Countries and Their Cultures*, ed. Melvin Ember and Carol R. Ember (New York: Macmillan, 2001), 2:1001–10.
3. This is not a uniquely Hungarian feature of national self-image. Indeed, among several others, the Croats and the Poles also hold that they are the bulwark of Western Christianity and civilization, while the Serbs are certain that they are the Western outposts of Christianity and civilization.
4. Hungarian American language use has been studied by a handful of scholars. For the best examples see Joshua A. Fishman, *Hungarian Language*

Maintenance in the United States (Bloomington: University of Indiana Press, 1966); Miklós Kontra, "Changing Names: Onomastic Remarks on Hungarian Americans," *Journal of English Linguistics* 23 (1995): 114–22; Kontra, Miklós, Introduction, in *Túl a Kecegárdán: Calumet Vidéki amerikai-magyar szótár* (Beyond Castle Garden: Hungarian-American dictionary of the Calumet region), ed. Kontra, Miklós (Budapest: Teleki Laszló Alaptivány. 1995); and Csilla Bartha, *A Kétnyelvüség Alapkérdései* (Basic questions of bilingualism) (Budapest: Nemzeti Tankönyvkiadó, 1999). *Túl a Kecegárdán* is a filled with rich examples of "Hunglish" or "Magygol," where speakers not only mix Hungarian and English in a rather unique manner but also make up new words by using, for instance, an English word with a Hungarian agglutinate, or an anglicized Hungarian word. The volume, edited by Miklós Kontra, as Zsolt Bánhegyi commented, "is a unique dictionary within Hungarian lexicography, a fine and rare example of language contact by prominent scholars, the late Professor Endre Vázsonyi and his wife Linda Dégh. Drawing upon tape-recorded interviews, the book preserves the now extinct language used by Hungarian immigrants who settled in Michigan in the early years of the 20th century"(Zsolt Bánhegyi, Bibliography Hungarica, Budapest: C3 Alapítvány, c.3 hu-scripta [web]).

5. However, Hungarians are no longer the largest group in Europe living outside the boundaries of their homelands. In the late 1980s massive migrations and refugee movements, largely due to ethnic cleansing, began in the entire Eastern and Central European region, the Balkan Peninsula, and the former Soviet Union.

6. As the following petition from the 1990s clearly shows, the attempt to convince the powers about the unjust treaty is still an ongoing concern among some Hungarian American immigrants:

> Dear Mr. President: I am writing to you in the name of many Hungarian Americans in the _____ area. This letter reflects our great concern regarding the lack of basic individual and collective human rights of Hungarian minorities in Slovakia, Rumania and Serbia. In many cases ethnic Hungarians in those countries are deprived of their homes, churches, tradition and culture, even the use of their own language. All this in order to achieve ethnic cleansing and total assimilation. The brutal oppression is forcing many Hungarians to flee their homeland of a thousand years. We

feel, and certainly history proves that the present dangerous situation in East-Central Europe was caused by the misuse of victory and lack of justice and moderation at the Paris peace treaties in 1920 and 1946 when one-third of the Hungarian population was forced to live under alien rule in clear violation of the Wilsonian doctrine of self-determination. We feel that the punishment and the retribution against Hungary was excessive. Dear Mr. President: In view of the sufferings and the drama which started in Sarajevo in 1914 and still continues, we Hungarian Americans respectfully ask you to act in behalf of the oppressed by using the political might of the United States and the moral weight of your high office. Furthermore, and in order to prevent further violence and to achieve a just and lasting peace in East-Central Europe, we beg you to review the Paris treaties and reorganize the region which, in our opinion, would greatly enhance your reputation as a true world leader. May God bless you. Attachments: 1,000 supporting signatures.

7. See Béla Gunda, "America in Hungarian Folklore," *Journal of American Folklore* 83, no. 330 (1970): 406–16, for a fascinating collection of peasants' sayings, lore, tales, and beliefs about "Amerika," particularly on the notion that Hungarians were the first people to greet Christopher Colombus in America.

8. Erdmann Doane Beynon, "The Hungarians of Michigan," in *Occupational Adjustment of Hungarian Immigrants in an American Urban Community* (Ph.D. diss., University of Michigan, Ann Arbor, 1933), 8, comments that the 1870 census was the first that distinguished Hungarians from Austrians, and it a gave a total of 3,737 Hungarians in what was then the states and territories of the United States.

9. While indeed they were poor, the newcomers did not hail from the very poorest stratum of Hungarian peasantry, because, even with the help of their families, the very poorest could not afford to pay for the passage to America. See Erdmann Doane Beynon, "Occupational Succession of Hungarians in Detroit," *American Journal of Sociology* 39 (1933–34): 600–610; Erdmann Doane Beynon, "Crime and Custom of the Hungarians of Detroit," *Journal of Criminal Law and Criminology* 25 (May–June 1934; March–April 1935): 755–74; Erdmann Doane Beynon, "The Eastern Outpost of the Magyars," *Geographic Review* 21 (1941):63–75; Endre Vázsonyi, *Túl a*

Kecegárdán: Calumet vidéki amerikai-magyar szótár (Beyond castle garden: Hungarian American dictionary of the Calumet region), ed. Miklós Kontra (Budapest: Teleki László Alapítvány, 1995); Éva V. Huseby, "Hungarians in Southeast Michigan: Reports of the ACLS-HAS Team Project," *Journal of Folklore Research* 21, no. 2–3 (1984): 243–45; Éva Huseby-Darvas, "Handmade Hungarianness: The Construction of Ethnic Identity among Elderly Noodlemakers in Michigan," *Hungarian Studies* 7, no. 1–2 (1991–92): 187–96; Huseby-Darvas, "Hungarians," 2:142–45; and Éva Huseby-Darvas, "The Search for Hungarian National Identity," in *Ethnic Identity: Creation, Conflict, and Accommodation*, 3d ed., ed. Lola Romanucci-Ross and George DeVos (Walnut Creek, Calif.: AltaMira Press/Sage, 1995), 161–95.

10. Gizella Szabó, an exceptionally articulate, friendly, warm woman, whose command of the English language is outstanding, was born in 1919 in the village of Komoro, Szabolcs County. Her mother first emigrated in 1902, but she returned to her natal village several times before she finally settled in Delray, Michigan, in 1938. Gizella followed her mother in 1940. She commented that a number of children in her village enjoyed the foods and occasional presents and privileges that came from parents who were circular migrants, but at the same time they also suffered from the periodic comings and goings of their parents. Yet this was a regular, familiar pattern for many; it was the only way they were able to eke out a viable living in Szatmár County before the First World War, and those who had a close relative in the United States were able to use this strategy in the name of family reunification even after the restrictive U.S. immigration laws of 1924.

11. See Malvina Hauk-Abonyi and James Anderson, *Hungarians of Detroit, Peopling of Michigan Series, Ethnic Studies Division* (Detroit: Center for Urban Studies, Wayne State University, 1977); Beynon, "Occupational Succession of Hungarians"; and Erdmann Doane Beynon, "Crime and Custom of the Hungarians of Detroit."

    Koma in this case means a multi-stranded relationship, often including the fictive kinship of co-godfatherhood, as well as fellow villager, a friend, a former neighbor, a person belonging to the same age group, even a person with whom one served in the military.

12. See Faye Smith, *Bits of Old Detroit*, no. 4: Hungarians, *Detroit Sunday Night* 2 (18 February 1922): 3; Hauk-Abonyi and Anderson, *Hungarians of Detroit*.

13. Lois Rankin, "Detroit Nationality Groups," *Michigan History Magazine* (1939), 3.

14. Cited in Beynon, "The Hungarians of Michigan," 12.

15. The following was published in "In and around Detroit in 1910: Historical Photographs and Text," Souvenir Album *In and Around Detroit 1910,* Holy Cross Parish, Delray, Michigan 1910: "In the suburb of Delray, at the intersection of Smith and Harvard Streets, is Holy Cross Church, which was founded in 1906 by the Magyars, who are the real Hungarians. The Rev. H. F. Klenner was the first rector. He secured the property upon which he has erected a fine building, which answers for the present as church and school, also a sisters' house and rectory. One hundred and twenty children are in attendance and are under the instruction of the Dominican Sisters from Adrian" (43). The photographs and text were published in 1910 in honor of the seventh Annual Meeting of the Catholic Educational Association, which met in Detroit, Michigan on 5 July 1910.

16. However, in "The Hungarians of Michigan" Beynon notes that "until the late 1890s French and Germans populated Delray . . . [and] much antipathy was shown [by them] against the invading foreigners [the Hungarians]. In time the . . . old inhabitants gave way and the entire Delray was abandoned by them" (9–10). In other words, the displacement of one ethnic group by another that occurred at the end of the nineteenth and the beginning of the twentieth centuries was similar to the one that occurred after the 1960s, when African Americans, Cubans, Puerto Ricans, and Mexicans displaced the Hungarian Americans of Delray. It is also similar to the current situation, in which Polish-Americans are being displaced from Hamtramck by Albanian, Bosnian, Macedonian, and other newcomers from the Balkan Peninsula.

17. Linda Dégh, "The Ethnicity of Hungarian Americans," *Congressus Quintus Internationalis Fenno-Ugistarum* 4 (1980): 255–90; Linda Dégh, "Survival and Revival of Folk Cultures in America," *Ethnologia Europeae* 2–3 (1968–69): 97–107.

18. Kálmán Káldor, ed., *Magyár Amerika Írásban és Képben* (Hungarian America in text and pictures) (St. Louis: Hungarian Publishing House, 1939), 193.

19. Erdmann Doane Beynon, "Migration of Hungarian Peasants," *Geographical Review* 27 (April 1937): 226.

20. During the Great Depression and particularly the Prohibition Era there was lucrative and apparently much needed smuggling going on between Windsor and Detroit. This was primarily but not only an ethnic enterprise, in which, among others, some Hungarian Canadians and Hungarian Americans were participating (see Beynon, "Occupational Succession of Hungarians," "Crime and Custom of Hungarians"). According to the stories I have heard and read, the center of this important "second economy" venture was Zug Island, between the United States and Canada in the Detroit River. The focus was alcohol, but people were also smuggled into the States. Beynon found that an illicit occupation, such as proprietor of a "candy store," so called because the speakeasies often had a few bags of candy sitting out as a "front," often brought more social prestige to the practitioner of that occupation than did working in a factory, and that eventually many of those who ran illicit businesses during the Prohibition opened legitimate ones with the profits made in the clandestine undertaking.

21. See Laura Fermi, *Illustrious Immigrants: The Intellectual Migration from Europe, 1930–1941* (Chicago: University of Chicago Press, 1971).

22. There were some efforts that went beyond lobbying. For example, a much-publicized 1931 flight across the Atlantic Ocean was financed by Detroit Hungarian American businessman Emil Szalay, while the pilots came from Budapest, sent by the Hungarian Ocean–Crossing Flyers Association. The airplane, named "Justice for Hungary," made record time, thereby beating the previous record held by Lindbergh. As Mrs. Pálos said, the flight and the name of the plane were "intended to call the world's attention to Hungary and to the unjust Trianon Treaty."

Another effort that went beyond lobbying was that of Louis Birinyi, who in 1924 appealed to the American people from Cleveland for justice for Hungary and for world peace in a self-published book in English entitled *The Tragedy of Hungary.* Birinyi wrote that Hungary was not punished for her involvement in the Great War because the Big Four never believed that Hungary was at fault. Neither did Trianon occur because of the nationality question, since it was generally well-known that Hungary was most kind to her non-Magyar nationalities. Throughout history, "Hungary was the defender of Christianity, the champion of democracy and the bulwark of civilization," so there was no reason to mutilate the country, yet there was a purpose. That purpose was, according to Mr. Birinyi, to allow the commerce of the world to be controlled by the Jewish financial magnates. Therefore, the author concluded, the Trianon Treaty might appear to be the horrible creation of the Allies, but in reality it was the brainchild of the ever-present Jewish world conspiracy. Unfortunately, it seems safe to assume that these and similar ramblings were not those of a single and isolated individual but representative of the classic scapegoating and blind fanaticism of many on both sides of the Atlantic Ocean, and that it was mutually reinforced by some individuals in the homeland as well as in the immigrant community. Furthermore, there are still some individuals today who think, write, and talk in terms frighteningly similar to the ones Birinyi used here.

23. Mrs. Pálos was unable to maintain this program after the mid-1980s due to a combination of factors, including poor health, financial difficulties, and problems after changes in the station's ownership and profile. However, between 1997 and 2001 there was a Hungarian-language radio program featuring the fine work of Mr. Zoltán Veres of Windsor, Ontario. The program was aired once a week, on Friday evenings between 9:00 and 10:00 P.M. on AM 680 WNZK. While it is dormant at the time of this writing, Mr. Veres told me that with the help of the University of Windsor he is planning to resume the radio program.

24. Mr. Zoltán Veres was born in Windsor, Ontario, in 1930. His parents, Louis and Eszter Veres, were born in the former Austro-Hungarian Empire, emigrated to Canada for economic reasons, and settled in Windsor, where Louis became a shoemaker. Zoltán Veres retired a few years before this writing from his position as superintendent of the Windsor Schools, and he continues to live in Windsor, where both he and his wife, Erzsike Veres, are very active and involved in Windsor's and Detroit's social and cultural life.

25. The great majority of DPs really did leave for these reasons. At the same time, however, undoubtedly there were also DPs who were eager members of the Hungarian Arrow Cross Party—the equivalent of the Nazi Party—or of the Hungarian Gendarmerie, and thus, as one Detroiter vividly expressed it, "there [was] plenty of innocent blood on their hands, and they had to get out to save their necks from the rope."

26. György Csepeli, personal communication.

27. Ibid.

28. Zsuzsanna Lórántffy was born in 1600 and died in 1660. The wife of ruler György Rákóczi the First, she actively supported Protestant causes, estab-

lished a number of schools, and was a well-regarded author.

29. Hungarian ethnographer Gyula Viga suggests that the *csiga tészta*, the distinctly snail-shaped egg noodle, is a specifically Hungarian dish. At the same time, he notes, apart from its special shape, this noodle is an integral part of the generally known "noodle-belt" of wheat-growing southern and east-central Europe. Often foodways are very slow to change, both because they belong to the particular stratum of culture that is formed very early in life, in the person's family of origin, which thus is the last to fade or disappear, and also, as Molly Schuchat suggests, because "the preparation and presentation of food becomes the most accessible of crafts." Gyula Viga, "A tésztakészítés sajátos eszköze a magyarságnál (csigacsináló táblácskák)" (Typical instruments of noodlemaking among the Hungarians), *Herman Ottó Múzeum Evkönyve* 28–29 (1991): 480; Molly Schuchat, *Hungarian Refugees in American and Their Counterparts in Hungary (Hungarian Food and the Interrelationship between Cosmopolitanism and Ethnicity)* (Ph.D. diss., Catholic University of America, Washington, D.C., 1971), *Anthropology Studies*, no. 18.

30. Zoltán Fejős, "Magyar ruha," "szüreti bál" és az amerikai-magyar etnikus kultúra néhány kérdése ("Hungarian dress," "grape harvest festival," and some questions about the Hungarian American ethnic culture), *Magyarságkutatás* (1987): 267–82; Zoltán Fejős, "Magyar szórványok multietnikus környezetben és az etnikus politika" (Hungarian ethnic groups in multiethnic environment and the ethnic policy), *Magyarságkutatás* (1989): 23–38.; Zoltán Fejős, "Chicagói magyarok temetkezési szokásai" (The burial customs of Hungarians in Chicago), *Vallási Néprajz 4* (1990): 279–315; Éva Huseby-Darvas, "'Wednesday Hungarians' and *Csiga*-Noodle Making in Southeast Michigan," *The Digest: A Review for the Interdisciplinary Uses of Food* 9, no. 2 (1990): 4–8; Huseby-Darvas, "Handmade Hungarianness."

31. It is important to note, however, that these csiga noodle making gatherings in Michigan are significantly different from those in Hungarian settings. In many settlements of north and east Hungary, primarily because of the lavish weddings staged for the young villagers, the preparation of the snail-shaped noodles often takes place in large groups that are composed of female participants of all ages. In Michigan, however, women under the age of fifty rarely attend these noodle making sessions. There are, of course, younger generations of immigrant women, but there does not seem to be

an upcoming generation of women with whom the social pleasures of making these noodles could be shared.

Contrary to the usual anthropological practice of giving pseudonyms, I am using the actual names of the participants here. The individuals are very proud of the fact that they are active in these noodle making sessions and they consider it a part of their very being, for some even their reason for being. Indeed, some of the women consider this social activity as the one important activity they do, and certainly the most eagerly anticipated one.

32. Mrs. Bíró was born in 1905 in the village of Matolcs, Szabolcs County. Juliska's father emigrated from the village in 1910, when she was not yet five years old. Juliska, with her mother and five siblings, followed fifteen years later, in 1925. Her father died in 1927, at which time her mother opened a "candy store" in Delray. Juliska started to work in a factory as soon as she arrived in Michigan and worked there for the next forty years. In 1928 she married István Mályi, a factory worker, and she gave birth to a daughter a year later. However, the marriage turned out to be "a very bad one," she said, so she divorced Mályi in 1935, and she married her second husband, Mihály Bíró, in 1942. Mr. Bíró was a widower from Transylvania, who at the time was raising a young daughter by himself. Juliska's command of English was practically nonexistent in the 1980s, nearly six decades after she moved to Detroit. She recalled that with one of her sisters she went to school to learn English, but "they laughed at us and said that they cannot understand us, so that we just stopped going after two weeks and never returned." Apparently she got along very well with only Hungarians. At the time of our meeting, in the early 1980s, Mrs. Bíró was one of the most respected members in a sizable csiga noodle making group, known as the best *gyúróasszony* (kneading woman), and in the many ethnic organizations to which she belonged.

33. See Csilla Bartha, A Kétnyelvüség Alapkérdései. .

34. See Hauk-Abonyi and Anderson, *Hungarians of Detroit.*

35. See the following Web site: The Hungary Page—More Famous Hungarians .htm

36. Galamb was born in a small Hungarian town, Makó, in 1881. After graduating from the Budapest Technical University, he worked in a wagon factory and later joined the biggest Hungarian automobile factory, in Arad,

Transylvania (now Oradea, Romania). At the beginning of the 1900s he studied manufacturing processes in the German Adler car factory. In 1903 he crossed the Atlantic to try his luck in the United States. He turned up in several cities, including St. Louis, Cleveland, and Detroit. He began to work for Ford in December 1905. Preliminary design work lasted six months. When Ford approved a part it was immediately made of wood, and thus the new Model T slowly took shape. Its most important part was the planetary gearbox, one of Galamb's most brilliant inventions. The Model T designed by Galamb was ready by 1908, and nineteen thousand cars were sold the next year. By adjusting the line, output was increased and unit costs reduced. By 1915, production reached one million units, and by 1927, when the production of the Model T stopped, a total of fifteen million had left the factory. József Galamb also designed the world-famous Fordson tractor and the ignition plug. During World War I he designed ambulance vans and light tanks, and he prepared for production Liberty aircraft engines. In 1927 he invented the modern and more elegant Model A to replace the Model T. In 1937 he was appointed as chief constructor at Ford, and he kept this position until his retirement in 1944. His daughter Gloria Galamb Albinak wrote to a biographer,: "to my surprise and pleasure I saw where you have my father, Joseph Galamb, listed as a famous Hungarian! Perhaps you would like to add his dates: 1881–1955 and the fact that he was at Ford Motor from 1906 to 1945, when he retired. He was Chief Engineer there, cut his teeth on the Model T and designed all Ford cars, tractors and airplanes until his health forced his leaving. He was a graduate of the Technicon, served in the Austro-Hungarian Navy stationed at Pola, came to the USA to attend the St. Louis World's Fair in 1903 [sic] and stayed."

37. According to the *University [of Michigan] Record* (16 October 2002): 2, in one of the many obituaries that appeared

> Kish also was one of the first proponents of an annual rolling sample, such as the American Community Survey, scheduled to replace the long form of the U.S. decennial census by 2010. In addition to his pioneering work in the theory and practice of survey sampling, Kish initiated a summer training program for foreign statisticians that now has two generations of alumni in more than one hundred countries. "More than any of his contemporaries, Leslie Kish improved the rigor and quality of census taking

throughout the world," said ISR director David L. Featherman. "An innovative statistician, his advice was sought from China to South Africa to Washington. His students populate the top echelons of statistical offices worldwide." Kish was born in 1910 in Poprád, then part of the Austro-Hungarian Empire, now in Slovakia. He emigrated to the United States with his family in 1925, settling in the Bronx, and within a year, his father died unexpectedly. His mother opened a pastry shop in Manhattan that was patronized by Eleanor Roosevelt, Gypsy Rose Lee, Eugene Ormandy and the violinist Fritz Kreisler. Kish worked during the day to help support his family, attending Bay Ridge Evening High School. In 1937, concerned about the threat of a fascist sweep through Europe, Kish volunteered with the International Brigade to fight for the Spanish Loyalists. Originally assigned to a medical unit, Kish quickly found his way to the front with a Hungarian battalion. "I met some Hungarians in a bar who told me, 'You don't have to go through basic training,'" he recalled. "'You go right to the front, we train you with the rifles, and you start shooting. And also, we have the best cooks.'" He was wounded in the battle for Huesca. He returned home in 1939 and, after attending night classes, graduated Phi Beta Kappa from the City College of New York with a degree in mathematics. He then moved to Washington, D.C., where he was employed first at the U.S. Census Bureau, then at the U.S. Department of Agriculture, where he joined a group of social scientists, including psychologist Rensis Likert, who were creating a survey research unit within that department. Again, his career was interrupted by war. In 1942–45, he served in the U.S. Army Air Corps as a meteorologist. In 1947, Kish moved to the University of Michigan . . . to found the Institute for Social Research. During his early years at Michigan, Kish combined full-time statistical work with the completion of an M.A. in mathematical statistics in 1948 and a Ph.D. in sociology in 1952. "Leslie had a tremendous appetite for life," said Robert Kahn, professor emeritus of psychology and co-author with John Rowe of *Successful Aging.* "It was a marvelous youthful quality, and it did not diminish as he aged. Appetite suggests food—and it is true that Leslie's motto as he traveled the world was, 'Anything a human being can eat, I can eat.' But his appetite for ideas and his capacity for friendship were even more remarkable. I treasure our 52 years of work and play together. I celebrate his long and productive life and only wish that it could have been longer."

Kish received many honors and awards during his career. He was named a
Russell Lecturer and elected president of the American Statistical
Association. He also was elected a fellow of the American Academy of Arts
and Sciences, the American Association for the Advancement of Science,
and the Royal Statistical Society of England. Kish's scholarly writing and
innovative research continued after his formal retirement in 1981. He traveled extensively, consulting on sampling and multinational survey design
with colleagues in the U.S. and around the world. He was elected an honorary member of the International Statistical Institute and the Hungarian
Academy of Sciences, and received an honorary doctorate from the
University of Bologna, Italy, on the occasion of its 900th anniversary.

38. Andrew Nagy's professional accomplishments are too many to mention,
but among the most noteworthy are his service as interdisciplinary scientist on the highly successful Pioneer Venus mission, which provided more
than fourteen years of continuous observations of the atmosphere, ionosphere, and solar wind interaction at Venus; his service as interdisciplinary
scientist on the Dynamics Explorer mission, which has provided valuable
observations of the terrestrial upper atmosphere, ionosphere, and magnetosphere; his service as co-investigator on a large number of very successful plasma and neutral gas experiments on various NASA and international
missions; and most recently his work on the POLAR spacecraft orbiting
Earth, the Nazomi mission to Mars, and the Cassini mission to Saturn. Nagy
has authored or co-authored more than two hundred publications in refer-
eed journals and has given approximately two hundred scientific talks and
seminars. He notes, "Our solar system is a vast laboratory, largely unex-
plored and unexplained. The similarities and differences in the behavior of
the environment of the various solar system bodies are wonderful learning
tools." His current research interests include the ionospheres of Mars,
Venus, Jupiter, Saturn, Europa, Io, and Titan; comparative planetology;
MHD modeling of the solar wind-planetary interaction; and low-energy
plasmas in the Earth's magnetosphere. Nagy is also a leading expert in terrestrial and planetary aeronomy. In the early period of atmospheric exploration, Dr. Nagy played a pioneering role in developing rocket-borne
instrumentation to sample the charged particle environment in the ionosphere. He participated in the development and testing of the first ground-

based Fabry-Perot interferometer to measure the 6,300 Doppler-temperature of atomic oxygen during the occurrence of sub-auroral red (SAR) arcs. He and colleagues developed early theories describing the diurnal and magnetic storm associated flows of plasma at midlatitudes. With colleagues in California, he developed a unique numerical modeling technique to study the aeronomical effects of charge particle transport in the upper atmosphere. These versatile techniques are so powerful that they have since been applied to such diverse subjects as the earth's ionosphere and auroras, the ionospheres of the inner and outer planets, auroras on Jupiter and Saturn, cometary environments, and heavy ion precipitation. Because of the relative simplicity of the techniques, they have also been adapted to form part of more complex numerical models of the ionosphere-thermosphere-atmosphere system being developed today. He has been awarded the NASA Public Service Award, and he is a fellow of the American Geophysical Union, a member of the International Academy of Astronautics, and a member of the Hungarian Academy of Sciences.

39. Father Vendel Pócsai also told me in 1989 that he knew of fourteen Hungarian households with twenty-six individuals who live in the Delray.

40. The sergeant said that many of the elderly don't trust banks and credit unions, and keep their money hidden in their houses. Men posing as representatives of Michigan Consolidated Gas, Michigan Bell, Sears and Roebuck, or other well-known organizations sometimes force their way into the houses of the elderly and rob them. This is what is known as "Gypsy Fraud," though I don't see the relationship between this type of crime and the Roma in the neighborhood, who are clearly also very much victims of the urban blight.

41. Jerry Hansen, "Why they called it Delray?" *Detroit Free Press Sunday Magazine*, September 1963.

42. Mr. Veres's is a nice and rather fitting image, not only because Buda and Pest were likewise two separate cities until the creation of Budapest from the three cities of Buda, Pest, and Óbuda in 1873, but also because they were likewise divided by a major and important river, the Danube, with the people of the two sides of the Danube relying on what both sides had to offer. This certainly holds similarities to the situations of members of the Hungarian communities of both Detroit and Windsor.

43. Actually, I believe that Mr. Veres might be underestimating here: There was

ongoing intercourse between the two border cities long before the 1930s, but travel became much easier when the Ambassador Bridge was completed and the Windsor-Detroit Tunnel was opened in the 1930s, and it followed that economic, social, and cultural exchange became more intense after this point.

44. Éva Huseby-Darvas, "Wednesday Hungarians and *Csiga*-Noodle Making in Southeast Michigan"; Éva Huseby-Darvas, "'Coming to America': The Dilemmas of Ethnic Groups since the 1880s," in *The Development of Arab-American Identity,* ed. Ernest McCarus (Ann Arbor: University of Michigan Press, 1994), 9–21.

45. Schuchat, *Hungarian Refugees in America.*

46. I was told that for the last few decades the members of this association have not really needed to have any actual connection with either Szabolcs or Szatmár County, which was the natal home of so many of the Hungarians in Michigan particularly from the first wave of immigration.

47. Also see Zoltán Fejős, "'A temető e csender árnyán, itt nyugszik egy vándor árván': Chicagói magyarok temetkezési szokásai" ("In this quiet shade of the cemetery, there lies an orphaned wanderer": Funeral customs of Hungarians in Chicago), in *Vallásosság és Népi Kultúra a Határainkon Túl* (Religiousness and folk culture beyond our borders), ed. Zoltán Fejős and Imola Küllős (Budapest, 1990), 279–315, on the funeral customs of Hungarians in Chicago.

48. I appreciate my student Lisa Tiger's help in looking at funeral customs among Hungarian Americans in Michigan.

49. Red, white, and green are the colors of the Hungarian flag. These three colors together and in that order are used on many Hungarian products, and are particularly relevant beyond the borders of Hungary, where the emphasis on Hungarianness becomes crucially important and most often expressed through items of material culture and foodways that are laden with conspicuous national symbols.

50. Between 1979 and 1982, when participating in Project ÁMEN, I interviewed scores of people over the age of sixty in the southeast part of the state. (Project ÁMEN—Hungarian acronym for Amerikai Magyar Emigránsok Néprajza, or Ethnography of American Hungarian Immigrants—was designed and directed by Béla C. Maday, and supported by NEA and other grants.) Then, in a study of Hungarian radio programs in the Detroit area, I

interviewed more than fifty people (Éva V. Huseby, "Ethnic Radio: A Study of Hungarian Radio Programs in Detroit and Windsor," in *Beyond Ethnic Boundaries: New Approaches in the Anthropology of Ethnicity*, Michigan Discussions in Anthropology, volume 7, edited by William Grover Lockwood [Ann Arbor: University of Michigan, Department of Anthropology, 1984], 1985). Between October 1984 and June 1985, with the generous support of NEA Research Grant NEA-RO-20663-84, I studied generativity among older women. Finally, field study in the summer and fall of 1990 was made possible by a grant from the Alcohol Research Center of the University of Michigan.

51. With the very kind permission of Mrs. Leleszi, I am using her actual name. The cover photograph depicts thirteen-year-old Mariska's arrival in New York Harbor on the SS *Europa* in 1930. The ship, she told me, made record time crossing the Atlantic. It crossed in four days from Bremen to New York. Another woman told me that when her parents came in 1907 on an old sailing vessel, it took thirty days to reach Ellis Island.

52. With the guidance of Dr. Yvonne Lockwood, curator of the Museum MSU, the Hungarian Arts Club generously helped Michigan State University's Museum to buy a very special cimbalom, a Gypsy musical instrument, from one of the musicians, who, according to his daughter, said that he needed the money for the kind of funeral he wanted to have. Shortly after getting the money he died, and he indeed had the type of lavish funeral for which he had hoped.

For Further Reference

Recommended readings are marked with an asterisk (*).

Agócs, Carol, James A. Anderson, Paul Gauche, and Bryan Thompson. *Ethnic Detroit in Maps.* Ethnic Studies Division Center for Urban Studies, Wayne State University and Southeast Michigan Regional Ethnic Heritage Center. Detroit: Wayne State University, 1975.

Bánhegyi, Zsolt. *Bibliography Hungarica.* Budapest:C 3 Alapítvány, c.3 huscripta (web), 1995.

Bartha, Csilla. *Adalékok a detroiti magyar közösség nyelvállapotához* (Data on the language situation of the Detroit Hungarian community). *Magyar Nyelv* 85, no. 2 (1989): 230–35.

———. *A Kétnyelvüség Alapkérdései* (Basic questions of bilingualism). Budapest: Nemzeti Tankönyvkiadó, 1999.

*Benkart, Paula. "Hungarians." In *Harvard Encyclopedia of American Ethnic Groups,* edited by Stephan Thernstrom. Cambridge, Mass.: Harvard University Press, 1980.

Beynon, Erdmann Doane. "The Hungarians of Michigan," in *Occupational Adjustment of Hungarian Immigrants in an American Urban Community.* Ph.D. diss., University of Michigan, Ann Arbor, 1933.

———. "Occupational Succession of Hungarians in Detroit." *American Journal of Sociology* 39 (1933–34): 600–10.

———. "Crime and Custom of the Hungarians of Detroit." *Journal of Criminal*

Law and Criminology 25 (May–June 1934, March–April 1935): 755–74

———. "Social Mobility and Social Distance among Hungarian Immigrants in Detroit." *American Journal of Sociology* 41 (1935–36): 423–34.

———. "Migration of Hungarian Peasants." *Geographical Review* 27 (April 1937): 214–28.

———. "The Eastern Outposts of the Magyars." *Geographical Review* 31 (January 1941): 63–78.

Birinyi, Louis. *The Tragedy of Hungary.* Cleveland: author, 1924.

Bognár, Desi. *Hungarians in America: A Biographical Directory of Professionals of Hungarian Origin in the Americas.* East European Biographies and Studies Series, edited by Desi K. Bognár and Katalin Szentpály. Mt. Vernon, N.Y.: Afi Publication.

*Dégh, Linda. "Survival and Revival of Folk Cultures in America." *Ethnologia Europeae* 2–3: 97–107.

*———. "The Ethnicity of Hungarian Americans." *Congressus Quintus Internationalis Fenno-Ugristarum* 4 (1980): 255–90.

Detroit Police Department, Fourth Precinct. Computerized Monthly Reports from the Statistics and Record Division, 1981–1988.

*Dreisziger, Nándor F., with M. L. Kovács, Baul Bõdy and Bennett Kovrig. *Struggle and Hope: The Hungarian Canadian Experience.* Generation: A History of Canada's Peoples Series. Toronto: McClelland and Stewart, 1982.

Fejős, Zoltán. "'Magyar ruha,' 'szüreti bál' és az amerikai-magyar etnikus kultúra néhány kérdése" ("Hungarian dress," "grape harvest festival," and some questions about the American-Hungarian ethnic culture). *Magyarságkutatás* (1987): 267–82.

———. "Magyar szórványok multietnikus környezetben és az etnikus politika" (Hungarian ethnic groups in multiethnic environment and the ethnic policy). *Magyarságkutatás* (1989): 23–38.

———. "Folklór és hagyomány a chicagói magyar szervezetek identitás alakításában" (Folklore and tradition in the identity formation of Hungarian associations in Chicago). *Varietas Historiae* (1989): 111–28.

———. "Chicagói magyarok temetkezési szokásai" (The burial customs of Hungarians in Chicago). *Vallási Néprajz* 4 (1990): 279–315.

*———. "The Hungarian-American Press and the Second Generation: Forms, Aims and Prospects." *Humanistika/Humanities. Znanstvena Revija* 3, no. 2 (1991): 517–32.

*Fermi, Laura. *Illustrious Immigrants: The Intellectual Migration from Europe, 1930–1941.* Chicago: University of Chicago Press, 1971.

Fishman, Joshua A. *Hungarian Language Maintenance in the United States.* Bloomington: University of Indiana Press, 1966.

Gans, Herbert. "Symbolic Ethnicity: The Future of Ethnic Groups and Cultures in America." *Ethnic and Racial Studies* 2, no. 1 (1979): 1–20.

Grácza, Dezső, and Margaret Grácza. *The Hungarians in America.* Minneapolis, Minn: Lerner Publishing, 1969.

*Gunda, Béla. "America in Hungarian Folklore." *Journal of American Folklore* 83, no. 330 (1970): 406–16.

Hansen, Jerry. "Why they called it Delray?" *Detroit Free Press Sunday Magazine,* September 1963.

Hauk Abonyi, Malvina. "Hungarians." In *Ethnic Groups in Michigan.* Volume 2 of the Peoples of Michigan Series. edited by James M. Anderson and Iva A. Smith. Detroit: Ethnos Press, 1983.

Hauk-Abonyi, Malvina, and James Anderson. *Hungarians of Detroit.* Peopling of Michigan Series, Ethnic Studies Division. Detroit, Mich.: Center for Urban Studies, Wayne State University, 1977.

Hauk-Abonyi, Malvina, and Mary Horvath-Monrreal. *Touring Ethnic Delray.* Field Trip Series, Tour Number 6. Detroit: Southeast Michigan Regional Ethnic Heritage Studies Center, n.d.

Hungarian American Cultural Center. *http://www.hungarianamericandetroit .freewebspace.com/index.html.* Accessed 21 March 2003.

The Hungary Page—More Famous Hungarians. *HipCat@Hungary.org.* Accessed 21 March 2003.

Huseby, Éva V. "Hear the Voices of Other Cultures." *Detroit Free Press,* 21 July 1982, 6B.

———. "Ethnic Radio: A Study of Hungarian Radio Programs in Detroit and Windsor." In *Beyond Ethnic Boundaries: New Approaches in the Anthropology of Ethnicity.* Michigan Discussions in Anthropology, volume 7, edited by William Grover Lockwood. Ann Arbor: University of Michigan, Department of Anthropology, 1984.

———. "Hungarians in Southeast Michigan, 5: Reports of the ACLS-HAS Team Project." *Journal of Folklore Research* 21, no. 2–3 (1984): 243–45.

Huseby-Darvas, Éva. "'Wednesday Hungarians' and *Csiga*-Noodle Making in Southeast Michigan." *The Digest: A Review for the Interdisciplinary Uses of Food,* edited by Yvonne Lockwood and William G. Lockwood. 9, no. 2 (1990): 4–8.

*———. "Handmade Hungarianness: The Construction of Ethnic Identity among Elderly Noodlemakers in Michigan." *Hungarian Studies* 7, no. 1–2 (1991–92): 187–96.

———. "Hungarians." In *The Encyclopedia of World Cultures,* edited by David Levinson. Volume 2. New Haven, Conn.: Yale University Press, 1992.

———. "'Coming to America': The Dilemmas of Ethnic Groups since the 1880s." In *The Development of Arab-American Identity,* edited by Ernest McCarus. Ann Arbor: University of Michigan Press, 1994.

*———. "The Search for Hungarian National Identity." In *Ethnic Identity: Creation, Conflict, and Accommodation.* 3d ed. Edited by Lola Romanucci-Ross and George DeVos. Walnut Creek, Calif.: AltaMira Press/Sage, 1995.

———. "Hungarian-Americans." In *American Immigrant Cultures: Builders of a Nation,* edited by David Levinson and Melvin Ember. Volume 1. London: MacMillan Reference Library, 1997.

———. "Hungary." In *Countries and Their Cultures,* edited by Melvin Ember and Carol R. Ember. Volume 2. New York: Macmillan Reference USA, 2001.

Hutchingson, E. P. *Immigrants and Their Children, 1850–1950.* Census Monograph Series. New York: John Wiley and Sons, 1956.

The Institute for the History of the 1956 Revolution *http://www.rev.hu/history _of_56/naviga/index.html* and *http://www.rev.hu/archivum/tanulforr.html.* Accessed 21 March 2003.

József, Attila. *"Hazám": József Attila minden verse* ("My homeland": József Attila's complete works). Budapest: Szépirodalmi Kiadó, 1980.

Káldor Kálmán, ed. Magyár Amerika Irésban és Képben (Hungarian America in writing and pictures). St. Louis: Hungarian Publishing House, 1939.

Kolakowski, Leszek. *Modernity on Endless Trial.* Chicago: University of Chicago Press, 1990.

Kontra, Miklós. *Fejezetek a South Bend-i Magyar Nyelvhasználatból* (Passages from the usage of Hungarian in South Bend). Linguistica, Series A Studia et Dissertationes, 5. Budapest: Institutum Linguisticum Academiae Scientiarum Hungaricae, 1990.

———. "Changing Names: Onomastic Remarks on Hungarian-Americans." *Journal of English Linguistics* 23, nos. 1–2 (1991–95): 114–22.

———, ed. *Túl a Kecegárdán: Calumet Vidéki amerikai- magyar szótár* (Beyond Castle Garden: Hungarian-American dictionary of the Calumet region).

Budapest: Teleki Laszló Alaptivány. 1995.

*Kósa, Lajos. *Land of Choice.* Toronto: University of Toronto Press, 1956.

Kovács, Ilona. *The Hungarians of the United States: An Annotated Bibliography.* Budapest: Folklore Tanszék, Eötvös Lóránd Tudományegyetem, 1981.

Lampland, Martha. "The Politics of History: Historical Consciousness of 1847–1849." *Hungarian Studies* 6, no. 2 (1990): 185–94.

Lengyel, Emil. *Americans from Hungary.* Philadelphia: J. B. Lippincott, 1948.

Office of Refugee Settlement. *Report to the Congress. Refugee Resettlement Program.* Washington, D.C.: United States Department of Health and Human Services, 1986, 1993.

Pulitzer, Paul. "The Hungarian Community in North America and the Realities of the 1990s." *Educator: The Newsletter of the American-Hungarian Educators Association* 11, no. 2 (1990): 1–4.

*Puskás, Julianna. *From Hungary to the United States, 1880–1914.* Budapest: Akadémiai Kiadó, 1983.

*———. *Overseas Migration from East Central and Southeastern Europe, 1880–1940.* Budapest: Akadémiai Kiadó, 1990.

*———. *Ties that Bind, Ties that Divide: 100 Years of Hungarian Experience in the United States.* New York: Holmes and Meier, 2000.

Rankin, Lois. "Detroit Nationality Groups." *Michigan History Magazine* (1939).

Sanders, Iván. "Bebörtönözött Nyelv?" (Imprisoned language?). *Valóság* 5 (1973): 90–95.

———. "Két világ között: egy amerikai magyar vallomása" (Between two worlds: Confessions of an American-Hungarian). *Valóság* 8 (1974): 84–94.

Schuchat, Molly. "Hungarian Refugees in America and their Counterparts in Hungary. (Hungarian Food and the Interrelationship between Cosmopolitanism and Ethnicity)." Ph.D. diss., Catholic University of America, Washington, D.C., 1971. Anthropology Studies No. 18.

Smith, Faye. *Bits of Old Detroit.* No. 4: Hungarians. In: Detroit Sunday Night. February 18, 1922 (2).

*Sugar, Peter. *A History of Hungary.* Bloomington: Indiana University Press, 1990.

Szent Kereszt Egyházközség 75 éves Jubileuma (Seventy-fifth anniversary issue of the Detroit Holy Cross Parish). Youngstown, Ohio: Franciscan Fathers Catholic Publishing Co., 1980.

Széplaki, József. *The Hungarians in America, 1583–1974.* Dobbs Ferry, N.Y.: Oceana Publications, 1975.

Török, István. "A Detroiti (Michigan Állam) Szent Kereszt Templom" (The Holy Cross Church in Detroit, Michigan.) In *Katolikus Magyarok Észak-Amerikában* (Roman Catholic Hungarians in North America). Youngstown, Ohio: Katolikus Magyarok Vasárnapja, 1978.

———. "A flinti (Michigan) Szent József Templom" (The Church of Saint Joseph in Flint, Michigan). In *Katolikus Magyarok Észak-Amerikában* (Roman Catholic Hungarians in North America). Youngstown, Ohio: Katolikus Magyarok Vasárnapja, 1978.

Tóth, Tibor. *Historical Album for the Dedication of the Hungarian Reformed Church.* Detroit: Pálos. 1941.

*Várdy, Steven Béla. *The Hungarian Americans.* Boston: Twayne Publishers, 1985.

*Vázsonyi, Andrew. "The *cicisbeo* and the Magnificent Cuckold: Boardinghouse Life and Lore in Immigrant Communities." *Journal of American Folklore* 91 (1978): 641–56.

Viga, Gyula. "A tésztakészítés sajátos eszköze a magyarságnál (csigacsináló táblácskák)" (Typical instruments of noodlemaking among the Hungarians). *Herman Ottó Múzeum Evkönyve* 28–29 (1991): 465–82.

Vázsonyi, Endre. *Túl a Kecegárdán: Calumet vidéki amerikai-magyar szótár* (Beyond Castle Garden: American-Hungarian dictionary of the Calumet region). Collected by Linda Dégh and Endre Vázsonyi and edited by Miklós Kontra. Budapest: Teleki László Alapítvány, 1995.

*Weinstock, S. Alexander. *Acculturation and Occupation: A Study of the 1956 Hungarian Refugees in the United States.* The Hague: Nijhoff, 1969.

Index